DEFIANT

PROFILES OF RESISTANCE

BRIAN DOOLEY

HUMANITAS
MEDIA

9781967494026 (Hardcover)
9781967494033 (eBook)

Book cover design by Alexia Garaventa and Tracy Aanenson
Book design by Alexia Garaventa
Map design by Rick Lebo

Manufactured in the United States of America

Published by
Humanitas Media
3288 Owasso Heights Road
St. Paul, MN 55126
www.humanitasmedia.org

Distributed by Simon and Schuster
www.simonandschuster.com

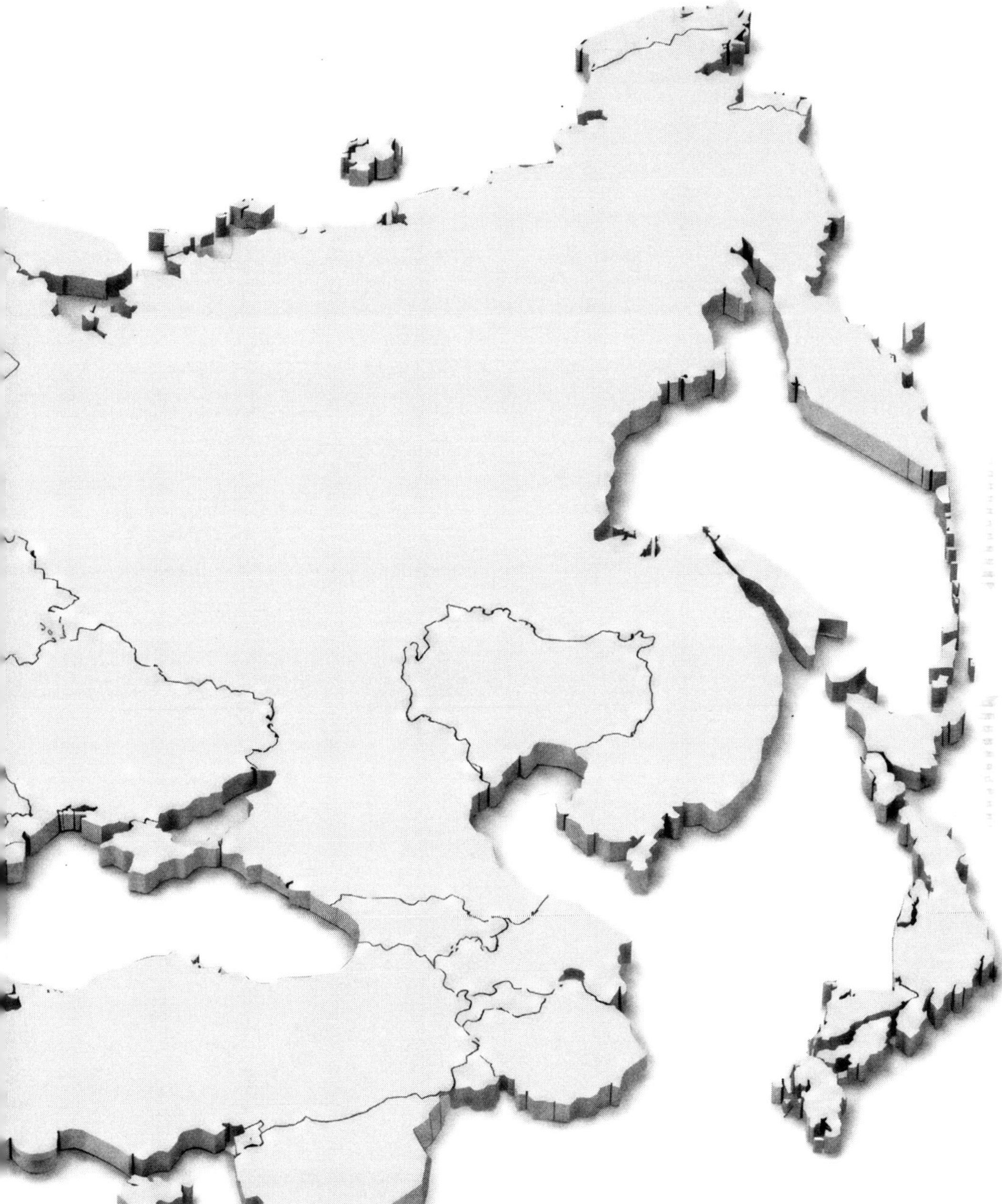

DEFIANT

PROFILES OF RESISTANCE

For Greta Dooley

CONTENTS

INTRODUCTION

I've spent decades reporting on human rights activists working at enormous risk around the world, but the ones who fascinate me most are those who take action without any experience, relevant qualifications, or previous interest in human rights work.

The people in this book show what's possible with imagination and willpower and a depth of courage they might not have known they possessed. Their examples offer encouragement to anyone reticent about taking first steps to help others. This sort of kindness in action is vital to countering today's crisis of growing state violence and repression, because it defies apathy and offers hope.

It is hard not to see that many of the world's democracies are poised at the start of a terrible new era, and that if things don't improve, the gains of recent years will be destroyed by a new surge of totalitarianism and hatred. But for those of us who remember a time prior to the 1990s, many of today's seemingly insoluble problems are familiar—so not all hope is lost.

In the 1970s and 1980s, much of Latin America was ruled by dictatorships, and an openly racist government held power in South Africa. In Eastern Europe, the Soviet Union was in control. In Western Europe, military generals governed Spain, Portugal, and Greece. In Northern Ireland, a violent conflict dominated everyday life for decades. These situations didn't improve on their own. Dictatorships didn't magically fall; the Soviet Union didn't simply collapse under its own weight. These regimes were brought down in part with the help of people working locally on their own or with others to undermine repression with defiant acts of kindness.

So, too, have those featured in this book defied injustice to shape a more hopeful future. I met and interviewed all these people in person in 2025, in either their homes, their offices, or coffee shops near where they live. I asked them why they rejected an easier path and refused to look away, why they resisted the temptation not to get involved. They are an eclectic mix, and some struggle to explain where their strong motivation to do good originates, but they have in common a willingness to act when most others won't.

All the stories in this book are from Europe. Of course, there are countless other examples elsewhere in the world. I think of Hassan Abd al-Rauf, a local shop owner in the Sudanese capital Khartoum, who ran a travel agency and a men's clothing store. When the Rapid Support Forces militia invaded his neighborhood in 2023, instead of escaping or complying with their orders to leave, he stayed. He walked around the deserted district, live-recording broadcasts on his Facebook page of unarmed civilians lying dead in the streets. He was detained for weeks before escaping the country.

I think, too, of the young volunteers I met during the 2019–20 Hong Kong revolution, treating injured protestors so they could avoid the risk of arrest at a hospital. I've met volunteers at similar underground clinics in Egypt and Bahrain, too, providing medical help to those in need while putting themselves at great risk.

In the interests of balance, I have not profiled more than two individuals from any one country, and only then if they were working on different issues. All decided to act in response to a crisis in their locality, and not because they studied human rights or were at loose ends and looking for a cause to champion. The veteran Irish civil rights leader Bernadette Devlin McAliskey said that by first joining local protests as a young student in the mid-1960s in response to discrimination in Northern Ireland, she became an "accidental activist." Many of those in this book have done so accidentally as well.

The first story in *Defiant* is about a former professional violinist, Nataliia Halunenko, who drives an ambulance to help civilians at the front line of Russia's war on Ukraine. I've driven with her to places under missile and drone attack and seen her courage firsthand. She explains how and why she started this lifesaving work and how she finds the energy to continue in the face of fear and exhaustion.

The Italian husband-and-wife team Gian Andrea Franchi and Lorena Fornasir treat and assist refugees braving the dangerous Balkan route through their home city of Trieste. Another married couple, Fidelma O'Kane and Cormac McAleer, from the north of Ireland*, have labored for years to put a stop to a planned gold mine.

All of those included here have a profound sense of compassion combined with courage to act with kindness in the face of often brutal opposition. The scientist Bülent Şık was put on trial by the Turkish authorities after he refused to keep silent about research showing dangerously high levels of toxins in food and drinking water in industrialized areas throughout Turkey. A group of tech-savvy activists in Poland faced a series of harassing court prosecutions after exposing the extent of the rampant homophobia in their country.

English lawyer Alastair Logan has battled for more than fifty years to expose how state officials framed eleven innocent people convicted of terrorism charges. I first met him in 1989, when he had already been working on the case for fifteen years. Here, he describes how he took on what seemed a hopeless cause and why he has stuck with it for virtually his whole career.

---

* The terms Northern Ireland and the north of Ireland are both commonly used. The former is more often used as a recognition of British rule in the region, the latter a geographical term, more likely to be used by those who dispute the legitimacy of British governance.

Iryna Fedoriv continues her fight against corruption in Ukraine despite receiving harassment and a bizarre death threat. She was also hit with lengthy court challenges after she led locals resisting developers' land grabs across an ancient neighborhood forest. Johanna Nejedlová from the Czech Republic recounts how her activism in Prague started spontaneously when there was an overwhelming response from strangers to something she posted on Facebook in 2015. From that start, a movement ignited that helped change how a country now views and prosecutes rape.

Hajrija Čobo from Bosnia is working in her post-conflict community to counter the new threat of gold mining to the environment. And a group of thousands of anonymous volunteers—the Baltic Elves—work clandestinely to counter myriad forms of incessant Russian propaganda in Lithuania and throughout Europe. Their work, like that of Anna and Zofia (their real names withheld), who repeatedly sheltered refugees in their home in eastern Poland near the Belarusian border, must be guarded with utmost secrecy.

My heritage makes me better placed to recount stories from Europe than those from other continents, but countless such stories are there to be told, and I hope someone tells them.

Defiant does not touch on my own activism, but, at the urging of the publisher, here's a bit of my background for context: I was brought up in south London in an Irish immigrant family in the 1960s and '70s. I had a classically poor but happy childhood with my parents and older sister, Chris.

When I was a kid, our home had no indoor bathroom or central heating, and the toilet was in the yard. My dad left school at the age of fourteen and, driven by memories of his own very real childhood poverty, worked seven days a week—as a mailman Monday to Friday and as a cabdriver on weekends. Mum worked as a cleaner in university dorms. Our house contained only a handful of books (and those few included one or two accidentally left behind in Dad's cab), but Chris often dragged me up the hill from our place to the local library when I was small, and there, a new world opened up for me.

At the nearby school—established for working-class Catholic boys identified at the age of eleven as supposedly bright—I usually ended up in the bottom half of the class academically, but I was happy enough playing for the school soccer team. As a teenager, I worked in a supermarket on weekends. In a nod to our Irishness, I played Gaelic football in London, and much of my teenage social life was based in Irish clubs in the city.

As I was growing up during the 1970s, the conflict in Northern Ireland loomed like a constant shadow over the Irish community in Britain as the Irish Republican Army (IRA) regularly bombed London and other British cities. Unpleasant things about Irish people were said to my parents at their workplaces, Irish families were under constant official and social suspicion, and there was always the chance of being arrested and accused of "being involved" in the conflict.

In 1981, having failed to get the exam grades needed for university and without many obvious prospects, I was shipped off without much discussion to live with my dad's brother in South Africa. I had met him only a few times before. Uncle Chris was a Catholic parish priest in Madadeni, a sprawling "Blacks only" township of around one hundred thousand people. Madadeni was one of the towns set up under the racist apartheid regime. Its residents had been forcibly relocated from other areas to live there, and the government's strict policy of racial segregation meant that only those officially designated as Black were allowed to be in the township at all.

Some exceptions were made for clergy, so while Uncle Chris was permitted to be in his parish and its surrounding area, I wasn't. In moving in with him at the age of eighteen, I began a year of living illegally in a Blacks-only area, working in the local school and clinic, and seeing up close the ugly violence of officially sanctioned racism and enforced poverty. I saw, too, how people regularly and quietly ventured into areas illegal for them to visit in order to bring food, medicine, and comfort to others or to organize against the racist regime.

Nelson Mandela and other anti-apartheid leaders were still in prison, but across the country, many thousands of other people undertook everyday acts of resistance, hiding dissidents on the run, helping them with false identity papers, and moving them around in the trunks of cars.

My only foreign experience prior to that absurd life was confined to visiting relatives in Ireland, and one afternoon school trip playing miniature golf in France when I was twelve.

My startling, eye-widening year in South Africa showed me how great people could be in responding to crushing odds—taking risks and breaking the law to help others in dire straits. A more orthodox path to university, a career in journalism, and work at nongovernmental organizations (NGOs) followed. Those years gave me the chance to meet some of the people in this book and to hear their stories of hope. I've since reported on people putting kindness into action, doing good at great risk to themselves in Gaza and Lebanon, in Bahrain and Kenya, in Egypt and Indonesia, and in many other places around the world.

All those gathered here are versions of Bernadette Devlin McAliskey's wonderful phrase "accidental activists," responding to injustice or violence with kindness and empathy. They range in age from a fourteen-year-old schoolgirl to a retired philosophy teacher approaching ninety. Some I met through my work as senior advisor to the United Nations Special Rapporteur on Human Rights Defenders, Mary Lawlor, between 2020 and 2023. One or two I knew from my work with the NGO Human Rights First. Some, like Alastair Logan, I've known for many years. Others were new to me, suggested by friends and colleagues as good candidates for this project.

None of those included knew each other, but when I described some of them to the others, there was often a chuckle of recognition at what they had done. When I told Hajrija, who campaigns to protect her local forest in Bosnia from pollution, about Turkish scientist Bülent—put on trial after making public the levels of toxins in the environment—she nodded with obvious admiration, laughed, and said, "Wow! That guy needs a truck to carry his courage."

Such people are often mistakenly dismissed as thrill seekers or adrenaline addicts, but they are simply prepared to do the right thing whatever the consequences. For these choices, for their defiance, those in this book have between them risked ostracization, abuse, jail, and death.

Friends and family have asked them to stop their activism, urging them to take an easier life, to put themselves first and stay out of trouble. Strangers often deride what they do, dismissing them as do-gooders, meddlesome amateurs, and virtue-signalers.

But what's wrong with doing good? There is much to learn from people who defy injustice and perform great acts of bravery and kindness in eras of repression. There is also much to learn from the defiance of those in the past. Many of those featured here are from communities that share a long tradition of resistance to oppression under Nazi or Soviet occupation, or both. While such historic resistance is often recounted as armies of underground local fighters helping to undermine, frustrate, sabotage, and eventually banish the occupation, it wasn't all about blowing up railway lines. On closer inspection, denying and ending Nazi occupation across Europe was a complicated, multilayered effort by hundreds of thousands of people countering violence and injustice with imagination and defiance.

Recent studies reveal that while many fought in the streets or deep in the countryside with the Maquis (French and Belgian resistance fighters), many more helped with quieter, subtler forms of dissent. French mechanics refused to maintain vehicles requisitioned by Nazi occupiers, and half a century later, as the Soviet Union teetered on the verge of collapse, East German gas station attendants refused to refuel Stasi vehicles.

Sometimes, when the moment of truth arrives, one has only a split second to decide. Life and death can hang in the balance. In her history of European resistance during the Second World War, Halik Kochanski recounts an incident in Warsaw, the Polish capital, in which a man named Jan Nowak was accosted and questioned by a plainclothes Nazi official outside a building where he was soon to meet a fellow resister. He spotted the brass plate of a dentist on the door beside him and responded that he had just been there for a procedure. The German rang the dentist's bell to corroborate Nowak's statement. "The unknown dentist, whom I had never seen and never would see had not hesitated for a second. She understood in an instant that someone's life was at stake," recalled Nowak, and so she lied and confirmed that he was indeed her patient.

Such traditions of daring and defiance are often passed along from one generation to the next. Some included here invoked childhood inspiration from older relatives. Turkish scientist Bülent Şık recalls how he was influenced as a boy by his uncle's principled high-risk work as a lawyer. Baltic Elf Giedrius said his spirit of defiance, of not being willing to accept the status quo, came from his grandmother. Lorena Fornasir tells how her mother worked with Italian partisans fighting the Nazis during the Second World War. She said her mother taught her the importance of "standing in the face of problems and finding the strength not to give in to indifference, individualism, and the destructiveness of the banality of evil."

This thread of nonviolent defiance can be traced back a long way. In 1880, rural people throughout the west of Ireland were dying from starvation. A man named Charles Cunningham Boycott in County Mayo had the job of collecting rents from destitute farmers for a wealthy landowner. In a campaign to resist extortionate rents, the farmers ostracized Boycott and refused to pay him. Their neighbors and their neighbors' neighbors quickly shunned him, and as a newspaper article at the time wrote, "Personally he is protected, but no woman in Ballinrobe would dream of washing him a cravat or making him a loaf."

Apart from bequeathing the term "boycott" to our language, the Irish locals in Mayo also provided an example for many others across the world to follow, including the US civil rights movement's 1955 campaign to boycott and desegregate the bus services in Montgomery, Alabama, after Rosa Parks's extraordinary act of defiance. She was arrested after refusing to give up her seat to a white passenger on a segregated city bus. A resulting boycott of the bus company lasted for more than a year, leading to the US Supreme Court ban on bus segregation.

Of course, many people naturally prefer not to get involved or to take sides when faced with grave injustice, instead tiptoeing along a difficult, neutral path. Polish writer Kornel Filipowicz was arrested and imprisoned in two concentration camps during the Second World War. His 1961 novel *The Memoir of an Anti-Hero* recounts the story of a character in Poland during the Nazi occupation who does whatever he can to keep out of the fight, to avoid siding with the oppressors or the oppressed. He spends the entire war trying to keep his head down and do nothing. It's a tempting response, hoping to stay safe by going unnoticed, to not get caught up in controversy or danger. All of those in this book could have taken that path, but, like many in Europe and elsewhere before them, when confronted with injustice, they decided to fight it.

In a memorable account in her book, *Tunnel 29*, Helena Merriman wrote of a courageous twenty-two-year-old East German student, Joachim Rudolph, who had recently escaped to the safety of West Berlin in September 1961. He was busy studying in his new dorm room when there was a knock at the door. He opened it to find three other students, who asked him to help them get people across from Soviet-controlled East Berlin to the freedom of the western side of the city. As we know, traveling through or over the infamous Berlin Wall was almost impossible. The three students were "asking him to tunnel back into the country he's just escaped to rescue people he doesn't even know," recounted Merriman. There were "so many reasons to say no, all more logical than the reasons to say yes." And yet Joachim finds himself giving an answer at once. He says yes. The youths eventually helped dozens of people to escape to the West. By taking on such a brutal and dangerous project, those young men digging tunnels risked long years in prison.

I asked each of the activists to explain their personal motivations for the work they do—why they said yes when so many others said no. For some, the answer is the same as for those defying Nazi occupation of the 1940s, for whom "resistance was a spontaneous reaction to oppression, of the soul even more than of the body." Others echoed the famed French Resistance activist Lucie Aubrac, who explained that in the early days of the German occupation, she didn't see her efforts as resistance but as a simple refusal to accept defeat, "a question of conscience."

In 2009, two neighbors knocked on Iryna Fedoriv's apartment door in Ukraine and asked her to help save an ancient local forest from illegal development. Despite the implicit danger from powerful oligarchs, she also found herself saying yes. Iryna reflected on doubts about what normality meant when she was confronted with so much opposition to her work: "You start to examine yourself, with all those people always against you. Sometimes you think deep down maybe you're the crazy one," she said.

Anna recounted how she hid refugees in her family home in eastern Poland when the authorities began to hunt those who had crossed over the border from Belarus. "The world is crazy, but I believe we should try to behave normally, and what's happening is not normal," she said. "If I end up in court for what I did, I'll know I stayed true to myself, and that is the most important thing for me." A refusal to conform with normal standards of morality and courage, as well as a willingness to be awkward and odd, are common characteristics of those in this book.

Historian Robert Gildea pondered the motivations of those in the French Resistance, asking: "Were they oddballs and eccentrics or idealists . . . moved by principles?" Leading resistor Emmanuel d'Astier de la Vigerie said, "I think you could only have joined the resistance if you were maladjusted."

Two years before his assassination in 1968, Dr. Martin Luther King Jr. talked about this idea of nonconformity and maladjustment:

> But I must honestly say there are some things in our nation and the world to which I am proud to be maladjusted and wish all men of goodwill would be maladjusted until the good society is realized. I never intend to adjust myself to segregation and discrimination. I never intend to become adjusted to a religious bigotry. I never intend to adjust myself to economic conditions that will take necessities from the many to give luxuries to the few, leaving millions of people smothering in an air-tight cage of poverty in the midst of an affluent society. I never intend to adjust myself to the madness of militarism and the self-defeating effects of physical violence.

Those in this book offer different but similar explanations for their motivations. Hajrija in Bosnia describes herself as "not normal. I'm very happy to be awkward, and at least I know it and accept it. I don't always want to go along with what everyone else wants, and it's a great strength." Nataliia, the violinist who drives an ambulance at the front line of the war in Ukraine, and who has saved countless lives over the last four years at enormous risk, said, "I don't see myself as a particularly kind person. . . . I just see that people need help and I can help. It's not complicated."

Keeping things uncomplicated and simple was another common characteristic of those featured. Some cite an early naivete as helpful, saying if they had known how hard things would become, they might not have started. Desperate to alert people outside Poland about homophobic council resolutions being passed across the country, Kamil in Kraków recalled "lying on my sofa with my laptop on my chest, emailing random politicians all over Europe."

Whatever their personal motivations, it is such people who—to paraphrase Dr. Martin Luther King Jr.—bend the arc of history toward justice. I think of a fifteen-year-old Swedish schoolkid who skipped her lessons and sat on the sidewalk outside parliament in Stockholm in 2018 to protest the destruction of the planet. Derided by most as an oddball, at best a naive do-gooder, Greta Thunberg was joined by a few others the next day, and more the day after that. A new social movement was born. Another ordinary person without much experience doing something remarkable.

While critics often dismiss those practicing kindness as do-gooders, outlaws, and eccentrics, some of the positive terms used to praise them are also unhelpful. I've long avoided describing such activists as "tireless" or "fearless" because many have told me it isn't helpful to suggest they're superhuman. The truth is that they get scared and exhausted just like anyone else, and pretending otherwise just increases the pressure on them. For some, there is social pressure not to admit that they are struggling emotionally and need a break.

As Alice Nah notes in her 2020 book, *Protecting Human Rights Defenders at Risk*, "Expectations that defenders were strong, brave, committed, and selfless made it difficult for defenders to share about their vulnerabilities." In Halik Kochanski's history of resistance to 1940s German occupation, she says, "Those who took part in the resistance were not supermen and superwomen, but were drawn from all walks of life. Some of the most heroic acts of resistance were performed by people who would not have been expected—even by themselves—to be heroes of any kind at all."

Not only is the heroization of people doing good and kind things unfair to them, but it also offers an excuse to those reluctant to act in a similar way, telling themselves and others that because they don't have such superpowers, they can't be expected to find courage or challenge injustice.

In 2015, I went to see my friend Ahmed Mansoor in Dubai. A peaceful critic of the Emirati government, he knew he was likely going to end up in jail. "Let's face it," he said to me over coffee, "sooner or later they're going to arrest me. There'll be a bit of a fuss, but it will hardly be a showstopper." Two years later, as expected, he was arrested, tortured, and sentenced to ten years in prison, where he remains, held in harsh conditions of isolation. When we met, I asked him why he didn't leave the country while he had the chance and why he stayed in such danger. "Sometimes it's like moving a mountain stone by stone," he said. "Many people privately say they agree with me. So I say to them, 'Come and join us. Courage is contagious.'"

This book is about everyday people like Ahmed, young and old, doing remarkable things. American anthropologist Margaret Mead is often quoted as having said, "Never doubt that a small group of thoughtful, committed citizens can change the world; indeed, it's the only thing that ever has."

Eighteenth-century Irish philosopher Edmund Burke is widely credited with saying, "The only thing necessary for the triumph of evil is for good men to do nothing." There's no evidence Burke ever said this, and the victory of evil over good takes more than other people's silence. But Burke did say, "When bad men combine, the good must associate; else they will fall, one by one, an unpitied sacrifice in a contemptible struggle."

My friend Serhii Prokopenko heads Gwara, an independent media outlet in Kharkiv, near the eastern front of the war in Ukraine. He reports stories of locals living through the war, including those taking risks to do good. On a trip to the front line near Izium a couple of years ago, we met Lyudmilla, a woman who had spent weeks digging out dozens of land mines by hand on her farm so she could plant vegetables, to be distributed by a women's business initiative in Kharkiv to help feed the city. As I drove us back to the city that night, he turned to me and said, "It's important to tell these stories. They give people hope, and hope brings energy."

He's right. We can change nothing without hope and energy, and everything with them. Those in this book show how this is possible. Here are their stories.

CHAPTER 1

NATALIIA HALUNENKO, UKRAINE

When Russia launched its full-scale invasion of Ukraine on February 24, 2022, thirty-year-old violinist Nataliia Halunenko was in her hometown of Svatove in the Luhansk region of eastern Ukraine. Within days, the Russian army had advanced rapidly westward across the region, occupying villages and towns with lightning speed. It even threatened to take the capital of Kyiv, in the middle of the country.

By March 8, Russian troops had already occupied Svatove, trapping Nataliia there with her parents. Russian soldiers soon captured her mother, who was a prominent journalist in the city, and held her for three days for interrogation.

"It was terrifying," Nataliia said. "When they released her, I decided to leave. And when I saw some friends and neighbors in Svatove choosing to side with Russian soldiers, something broke inside me and made me more determined to get away."

She explored ways to escape.

"There were drivers who took people out for money. You could go through the occupied territory, across the border into Russia, and then leave Russia and go into Europe, but it was dangerous, long, and expensive. I decided on another route—also dangerous, but faster," she explained. "At that time, the demarcation line between the armies was at the town of Pechenihy, where there is a dam. Ukrainian and Russian troops faced each other across the dam. The driver took us through the only possible road, via Kupiansk, to Pechenihy. I was traveling with another woman and a guy. We had to pass through twelve Russian checkpoints. Some we went through without incident; at others we were held for a long time, and Russian soldiers abused us verbally."

The road was so damaged, the car could only get to within a mile and a half of the dam, and then she had to walk.

"There were a lot of people trying to cross," Nataliia recalled. "You could leave only at certain hours on certain days. Some people were carrying suitcases, bags, and pets. Some of the animals ran away into the bushes, and it was impossible to go after them because the surrounding land was mined. I had only my backpack and my violin. When we crossed the dam, we were put on a bus to Kharkiv and given a hot meal."

Once there, Nataliia was free to settle anywhere in western Ukraine or to continue on to a place of greater safety in Europe, as millions of Ukrainian women and children did. (Men between the ages of eighteen and sixty were generally not allowed to leave the country.) Nataliia chose to stay, basing herself close to the front line in eastern Ukraine. She began volunteering with her sister in a food kitchen in Ukraine's second-largest city, Kharkiv, which is about the size of Philadelphia and just twenty miles from the Russian border.

This abrupt change meant Nataliia had to put her promising musical career on hold.

She had previously spent three years working as a violinist in India and had planned to move back there to restart her life as a musician. Although classically trained, she played mostly popular music at weddings and lavish corporate events and thrived in the high-octane adventure of India's music scene.

"Music was everything to me, my life, my passion. In India we played a lot of Bollywood tunes, and so it took a while to adjust to the new music, but I loved it," Nataliia said, laughing, "though I don't miss playing the *Titanic* theme tune over and over again."

She had hoped to return to that life of crisscrossing India, playing gigs all over the country, but the Russian invasion changed everything. By the summer of 2022, she was in Kharkiv, packing humanitarian aid and food parcels to be taken around the city and to communities right at the front line.

Kharkiv is a hard, gritty city with a reputation for endurance. During the Second World War, it was captured by Nazi Germany in late 1941, taken by the Soviet army in February 1943, and recaptured by the Germans a month later before finally being retaken by the Soviets five months after that.

In Russia's lightning-fast invasion of Ukraine in February 2022, the city looked like it was on the brink of being surrounded and captured. Tens of thousands of locals fled by rail and road. By that summer, when Nataliia arrived, Russian soldiers were camped on the outskirts of the city, constantly bombarding it with artillery shells and other missiles.

Kharkiv's infrastructure of shops and transport had largely shut down, the streets were nearly empty, and hundreds of people were living in the metro stations, having been bombed out of their homes and staying underground to survive the missiles.

Many locals remaining in the battered city relied on getting food, medicine, soap, and other necessities from volunteers like Nataliia. She was helping Kharkiv to survive, making a difference, but she felt it wasn't enough.

"At first I was making food parcels for people living on the front line," she said. "Then I agreed to help deliver them."

Packing food parcels in a city constantly pounded by shells was risky; taking them to civilians living at the very front was choosing to do something much more dangerous. Nataliia agreed to join a Polish volunteer to deliver food in December 2022 to the city of Bakhmut.

"It was my first trip to such a frontline city," she said. "I didn't really understand how many streets were destroyed or how much shelling there would be until I got there. We took medical supplies and food for people there and offered to evacuate anyone who wanted to leave. People were just huddled together in cellars, a dozen in some places, a couple of dozen in others, hiding from the bombing and waiting for the food we brought them. We took an older guy out who wanted to leave—he couldn't move much because he had a problem with his leg, so we took him with us."

Two months later, she went to Avdiivka, whose name has been burnt into the history of the conflict as a place of extreme brutality and danger. Russia's assault on the city lasted several years, and by the time it was finally captured in February 2024, the city had been reduced to rubble.

When Nataliia went there in February 2023, Avdiivka was still an urban battlefield, with many thousands of casualties in both armies in the grinding street-by-street conflict. Hundreds of civilians were also killed and injured, and many others were trapped by the bombings, too scared to make the journey out.

These experiences changed her. Nataliia decided more of this dangerous but vital work was what she needed to do. She began to take medical supplies and humanitarian aid along as she ventured into the most frightening areas of the eastern front.

"In Bakhmut, when you leave the van to deliver boxes of aid, you find yourself running, running all the time, because the explosions are all around you, sometimes only twenty yards away," she said.

I first met Nataliia when we were in an ambulance delivering medical supplies to the frontline city of Kupiansk in November

2023. Sitting in front of me with her trademark orange hair glowing against her flak jacket, furiously puffing on a vape, she turned to shout to me over the blaring Ukrainian rap music. We were slaloming at high speed through the deserted streets under bombardment.

"The artillery attacks continue all day. It's pretty random; anything here can be hit at any time," she said.

The shelling was almost constant, with black and white plumes of smoke rising on either side of the roads as missiles exploded. It was a rough ride for a while, and we hung on to what we could inside the ambulance as the wheels skidded and slipped in the mud.

We brought medicine to people living in high-rise apartment buildings who were unable to walk or to get down the many steps to the outside. The city's electricity had been cut in the bombardments many months before, and the buildings' elevators no longer worked.

"Some people just can't leave," she told me as we walked up the stairs of a battered apartment block. "Many old or infirm people stay in their homes, often with a family member to look after them. Some are just more afraid of leaving than staying."

As we talked, the ambulance's radio crackled with a warning that the small bridge we were heading for was being shelled. It was obliterated just before we arrived. An extremely close call. We managed to cross another bridge, even though it had been partly destroyed.

Nataliia has become used to this level of danger. It's how she has lived since Russia launched its full-scale invasion of Ukraine.

Nataliia and I have met several times since our first encounter in the ambulance. She's an expansive talker over coffee, gesturing rapidly with her hands. Despite everything, her default expression is a grin. As a teenager, she thought about joining the police, training as a musician, or even going into medicine.

"We didn't have the money for me to study medicine, but I guess now I'm doing it anyway," she said, laughing. In fact, she has become a trained ambulance driver and an expert in tactical medicine. "It's so different from anything I knew before. But what surprised me the most was that anyone, even somebody with no medical background, can learn to save a life. You don't need years of schooling to make a difference—you just need the will to act," she said.

Sometimes, she makes the long journey west to Poland to pick up a donated vehicle and then drives it a thousand miles back across Ukraine to the eastern front. When she arrives back in Kharkiv, there is never time to rest before moving on to the next crisis. Her life has run on constant surges of adrenaline, a force she said has shaped her since childhood.

"I've always been like this, you know: Go! Go! Go! Go! Go! I just get so bored in one place when I don't move; it's not for me. I just can't help it; it's in my blood, you know, to go for adventures," she said. "I was constantly doing things as a kid—regular school and then music school, playing on the street in those 'Soviet spaces,' the communal squares, the basic public playgrounds, of course with no internet."

She recalled singing in a punk band called Red River, after a river in her home city of Svatove. The band played a range of popular covers, as well as songs they wrote. She played her violin in the band, too, a bit of a breakthrough on the punk scene.

"Plenty of people coming to watch us had never seen a violin in real life and were fascinated. The kids stared at it and wanted to touch it," Nataliia said.

Always active, she also played volleyball at a professional level for a few years, before switching to karate, which she liked better.

"Here, doing this humanitarian work," said Nataliia, "I can use that energy to help people. And not everyone can do it, not everyone has the mind for it."

It takes a certain mindset and a strong sense of self to drive knowingly into extreme danger. "Going into a town being bombed, I don't feel that scared," Nataliia said. "I'm focused on what needs to be done. And when I'm there, I'm just concentrating on doing what I need to. You just try to keep quiet because you need to think what to do if a rocket hits your vehicle—how will I get out? Or what will I do if the car gets destroyed?"

It has been essential for Nataliia to stay calm for the sake of the people she has evacuated, who are vulnerable and often deeply traumatized.

"I've seen what happens when one person starts to panic—it's contagious and very, very dangerous. So you need to think, focus, and stay calm all the time. I realized after a while that I can maintain my self-control, and I'm lucky because it's natural for me," she said. "I know that not everyone can do this, but I can, so I feel I should do this work that others can't. I don't get that scared in these places. Yes, this is dangerous, and it is tragic, but somebody needs to do it, and who else is there, you know?"

The demand for volunteers willing to do this life-threatening work has been high. Along the hundreds of miles of the front line, vulnerable civilians need food, medicine, clothing, and other basics to survive. Many others want to be rescued from the shelling and fighting and to be taken to relatively safe places like Kharkiv, although that city has been attacked regularly, too.

Late in 2022, the Ukrainian military pushed back the Russian advance and reclaimed much of the area under Russian occupation. But a new Russian offensive in the summer of 2024 made slow but steady gains over the following year, bringing Russian troops to within twelve miles of Kharkiv. Faced with the loss of more territory, the Ukrainian army launched a conscription drive in April 2025.

Many men between the ages of twenty-five and sixty, who had been doing the kind of volunteering work Nataliia did, were drafted. This meant that the burden of this dangerous work has fallen more onto the shoulders of men over sixty and women. It has been a relentless, exhausting challenge, with people calling daily for help or to be evacuated, especially from communities under fire or where there are street battles.

Nataliia said she is usually "concentrating so hard" when she's in areas being bombed that she doesn't feel afraid. It's when she's leaving those places that the "fear" creeps in.

"Things can change minute to minute. While you're right at the heart of the war zone, you're without internet and can't get updates from anyone, so when you leave, you never know if the road that was safe on the way in is going to be safe on the way out. I have been very close to being killed," she said. "It's a possibility on every trip."

But Nataliia has thought about death only in the context of her family—that it "doesn't matter" to her but would be "very sad" for her mother, father, and sister.

"I didn't tell them I was going to Avdiivka. That would just be more stress for them," she said.

For those like Nataliia living these extremely dangerous lives, the pressure eventually takes its toll. At the end of every trip to the front line, she tries to relax, but there are always more people in desperate need of help.

"You have no rest; there's no break, you know, and you're tired," she said. "And you take the pieces of yourself, you know, and put yourself back together again every morning, ready to go again."

After three years of intense work in the war, something finally gave way for Nataliia.

"I got sick, like a depressive episode where I didn't want to get up, or to pick up any calls from anyone," she said. "So now I've learned to see the warning signals and force myself to rest. When I wake up in the morning and think, 'I hate this, I don't want to do it, I don't want to speak with anyone,' then I understand that I need a rest, because if I don't stop, I will burn out."

Nataliia said she is far from the only volunteer who has struggled with exhaustion. Recognizing it is key. "There are lots of volunteers here who reach a moment where they just can't carry on," she said. "I don't want that, so I take a rest, just a few days now and then."

She hasn't found any special cure for the extreme stress she's faced. Like anyone after a long day at the office, some TV and a good drink have helped.

"I watch TV shows and maybe have a few beers. It's my style to go nonstop, but I have to rest sometimes. My nickname is Ulcer because I'm so intense—I worry all the time and worry other people all the time," she said, smiling. "For all my resilience, I'm a difficult character and can be a bit rude. Sometimes people find it hard to communicate with me for a long time."

I've known her for several years and respectfully disagree.

"But I like my chaotic mind," she said.

Nataliia has helped save countless lives in more than four years since Russia's full-scale invasion of Ukraine. This work has given her, as she put it, "a purpose, a new life, a new way to be. Not the life I imagined or wanted, but the life I have now. It feels like what I should be doing while the war is on."

Her life in India seems a long time ago, although she still gets messages from music agents there asking her if she's available to play in the coming week. "They haven't heard things have changed for me a bit," she said.

Despite her efforts, Nataliia said she doesn't see herself as a "particularly kind person." She laughed, "I mean, I'm not evil, I guess. But you know, I'm hard to live with. I don't know how to explain it."

She has considered joining the military, but for now continues to provide medical supplies to dangerous areas. She also teaches tactical medicine courses along the front line.

"The teaching is a bit of a challenge," she said, "but it reminds me of performing as a musician. I mean, sometimes half the people in the medical class or in the music audience might not be that interested and are there in the class because they've been told to be there or in the audience because friends made them come. My job is to reach the half who aren't interested, who aren't sure they want to be there, and make them interested."

Much of Nataliia's work has involved evacuating civilians living under bombardment. But sometimes when she makes the dangerous journey to reach them, they are reluctant to leave their homes, even though they could be killed.

"If we get to somewhere being bombed and people have changed their minds and say they don't want to leave, I first ask people nicely, and then again politely," she said. "I explain we are volunteers. We've risked our lives to come and get them. If they're still hesitating to leave, sometimes they need a verbal slap to persuade them to come with us. I don't know if that's kind. It's intuitive, I guess. Some people need gentle words, and others need harsh words, and I can tell what people need to hear."

By late 2025, Nataliia had educated herself enough in tactical medicine to qualify as a full-fledged instructor.

"It's become really important in my life," she said. "I love it. I've taken lots of courses, read so much about it, and learned from many experts. I am also in a rapid response group. We go immediately to the scene of a missile attack in Kharkiv City to provide first aid to civilians."

On January 2, 2026, Nataliia was in Kharkiv visiting her parents. Her father had finally managed to leave the occupied city of Svatove and make it out, via Russia and Belarus, to unoccupied Ukraine. He had arrived in Kharkiv two weeks earlier. It was the first time the family had been able to spend the holidays together for several years.

Around 3:00 p.m., Nataliia felt the walls of their apartment shaking. She looked across at her father. He said it was probably just a door slamming upstairs, but she had been close to too many explosions not to recognize the sensation of energy coming from a bomb.

Nataliia was right. Two large Russian missiles had hit a residential building in the city center not far from where she was. Despite the freezing temperatures, she went outside and rushed toward the sound. Within minutes, she was one of the first on the scene.

"I was just in normal gym clothes, not dressed for an emergency," she said. "Several buildings were in flames, and so of course there is that immediate risk of sudden electrical fires and gas explosions, so anyone still in there was in real danger."

The Russian military is known, too, for using a double-tap tactic—firing missiles at the same target fifteen or twenty minutes after the first attack, hoping to hit firefighters and other first responders arriving at the scene with a second barrage.

I caught up with Nataliia over coffee a few days after the attack in Kharkiv. She told me she knew the dangers of immediately arriving at the site of a bomb strike but did it anyway.

"There was smoke everywhere, large chunks of concrete falling, the whole area devastated," she said. "I saw two elderly women, a mother and daughter, trapped in their apartment on the fourth floor of a damaged building. I helped force open their front door and got them out."

Despite the severe cold, Nataliia spent the rest of the day helping the emergency services and returned in the following days to continue the search and rescue efforts. Six people were found dead in the rubble, including a three-year-old boy, and many injured.

"When I heard the rockets hit, of course I had to go," she said, shrugging. She took a moment more to consider her motivation. "Maybe that's kindness, I don't know. I see that people need help and I can help. It's not complicated."

This volunteering has given Nataliia a good sense of who she is.

"It's exhilarating and can give me similar feelings to those I had performing as a musician," she said. "But I'm not that same Nataliia who was playing the violin in India. In some ways, I'm an uglier version of her. Before I was all about emotion, music, and beauty. Maybe all that emotion is still inside me, sleeping somewhere, I don't know. But I don't want to go back to that life."

CHAPTER 2

ANNA AND ZOFIA, POLAND

In late 2021, a family living near Poland's eastern border began sheltering migrants who had crossed into the country from Belarus. It was a dangerous move, carrying all sorts of risks, and they had to keep silent about it. Neighbors, colleagues, and school friends couldn't know. Being exposed could mean prison, and possibly still does. For that reason, I'm not using their real names here or the real names of those they helped. Sometimes, helping other people has to be done in secret.

Anna had been living in a house on the edge of the vast Białowieża Forest with her husband, her twenty-year-old son, and her fourteen-year-old daughter, Zofia, for years. They led a quiet life, nurtured by a spectacular natural sanctuary featuring over 250 species of wild birds and countless other animals and blessed each evening with some of Europe's most stunning sunsets.

The Polish border with Belarus, a former Soviet state still closely allied with Moscow, runs right through this primeval forest that once covered most of Europe. Known for its extensive biodiversity, thick undergrowth, and swamps, the dense Białowieża

Forest is a UNESCO World Heritage Site and offers habitats for elk, wolves, wild boars, lynx, beavers, and otters. It's home to the largest free-roaming population of European bison and is a bird-watcher's paradise.

"We're only 120 miles from Warsaw, but people from there think we are living at the edge of the world," Anna said. "Life moved slowly here, without any rush."

Then, in 2021, the forest's tranquility was shattered. The Belarusian government opened a new migration route through the forest, luring many people fleeing war and persecution in the Middle East and Africa with false promises of an easy passage into the European Union. This turned the region into a geopolitical battleground, with thousands of migrants caught in the middle and treated as ammunition.

A year earlier, Belarusian President Alexander Lukashenko, Europe's longest-serving leader, had rigged the election to secure a sixth term, and unprecedented mass protests had erupted across Belarus in response. The authorities violently suppressed the protests, arresting and torturing thousands and throwing opposition candidates in prison.

Not even dissidents abroad were safe. In May 2021, Belarus used a fake bomb threat to force a Ryanair flight carrying exiled activist Roman Protasevich to divert to Minsk. As soon as it landed, the police stormed the plane, arresting Protasevich and his girlfriend. In response, the EU slapped new sanctions on Lukashenko's regime and banned Belarusian airlines from flying over EU airspace.

A few months later, Lukashenko exacted his revenge, using the border with the EU as a weapon. In a carefully orchestrated campaign, his government offered visas and flights to people from Iraq, Afghanistan, Syria, Lebanon, and beyond while spreading false information on social media about the ease of crossing into the EU. Tens of thousands of people were lured to

Belarus's borders with Poland—and, to a lesser extent, to those with Latvia and Lithuania.

Belarusian border guards even escorted migrants to the edge of Polish territory before abandoning them in the two-mile-deep forest between the two countries. Initial feelings of hope for a new life gave way to fear and desperation as many, including children and pregnant women, struggled to survive.

Then-Prime Minister of Poland Mateusz Morawiecki called the crisis "a new type of war in which people are used as human shields" and said it was the first time in thirty years that Poland's border had been so "brutally attacked." The real mastermind, he said, was Russian President Vladimir Putin, Belarus's main supplier of political, financial, and military backing. Russia denied any involvement, but the ensuing chaos clearly served Putin's goal of destabilizing the EU.

For Anna and her family, everything changed that year.

"Living at the edge of the forest had been like a paradise. And then more and more people started to arrive. We were all shocked. For me, what people called an immigration crisis was the sort of thing that was happening in the Mediterranean, with people dying in the sea," she said. The limited way Anna pictured an immigration crisis wasn't surprising. According to the UN, since 2015, thirty-four thousand people have been reported to have died or gone missing while trying to reach Europe by sea, with the actual number likely to be much higher. Many desperate refugees are crammed onto dangerous boats that frequently capsize, drowning their passengers.

"I didn't think that could happen here," noted Anna.

International law forbids states from returning asylum seekers to a place where they face danger, but in reality, many countries do so. In October 2021, Poland amended its laws to allow authorities to push back migrants from a restricted border zone and ban them from reentering for up to three years, often without assessing their asylum claims. These measures were widely criticized for violating EU and human rights law, and a Polish court later declared parts of the law illegal.

Polish border guards have routinely and violently pushed many migrants back into the forest, where they soon encountered Belarusian forces bent on pushing them back toward Poland. Forced back and forth, migrants—including families with young children—have spent weeks wandering through the undergrowth, frightened of the wolves and the swamps, desperately hungry, and often ill.

Some migrants said Polish forces routinely beat them with batons. A BBC News report revealed the use of tear gas and water cannons. Accounts about the behavior of Belarusian border guards are even more harrowing. They include torture, rape, extortion, and even killings. A thirty-year-old Yemeni man told Human Rights Watch that Belarusian guards forced him and three others from Yemen and Iraq to stand in freezing water up to their knees before making them swim to Lithuania at gunpoint. One man drowned, and another was swept away and never found.

The Białowieża Forest has long been a site of persecution. During the Second World War, in June 1941 in Białystok, the city closest to the forest, hundreds—possibly thousands—of Jews were forced into a synagogue and burned alive by Nazi forces. Three weeks later, in Jedwabne, about forty miles farther to the wast, hundreds more Jews were killed after being herded into a barn that was set alight by local Polish collaborators. Hundreds of Jews who managed to escape the massacres scattered into the Białowieża Forest, where they were forced to forage for food and water while avoiding recapture and the unwelcome attention of wild animals.

Now the forest has again become a refuge for those trying to survive. Polish authorities have reported stopping one hundred thousand attempted crossings from Belarus since the fall of

2021—including thirty thousand in 2021 alone—but there is no reliable data on how many people made it into Poland.

Many locals living in and near the idyllic forest were startled at what was happening. Families from Syria wandered through their gardens, and exhausted Afghans stumbled into their villages.

Some locals pretended not to notice. Others reported the migrants to the police or border guards, hoping to see them returned across the border. But some people, horrified at the violence of the Polish authorities and at the prospect of migrants starving or freezing to death in the winter, began to help. They would venture into the forests with life-saving provisions—food, clothing, and medicine—and deliver them to migrants hiding in the trees.

By September 2021, experienced human rights activists in Poland had started to organize shelters and supplies and arrange transport to take migrants to other places in Poland. The work came at huge risk.

That same month, the Polish government declared a state of emergency, barring most nonresidents, including aid workers, medics, and journalists, from entering a two-mile-wide exclusion zone along the border with Belarus. This effectively criminalized humanitarian activities, such as providing food, shelter, or transport to migrants without official authorization. The formal exclusion zone ended in July 2022, but access to the border forests remains restricted due to police and border guard control. As a result, many aid workers and journalists have had to operate discreetly, communicating only via the secure messaging app Signal. Idle chitchat about their efforts is forbidden.

In the fall of 2021, I traveled to Poland to meet people secretly providing medical care. The underground clinics treated hypothermia, dehydration, and other conditions in people too afraid to go to hospitals. Exposure could mean being spotted by authorities and pushed back across the border into Belarus.

Anna was not, at first, part of the network helping people who had crossed the border, and she had no experience working clandestinely. But the situation shook her.

"To me, it was unbelievable that something like that was happening in Poland," she said. "And then there was some post on Facebook, from a group of so-called Real Polish Patriots, who said they wanted to get organized and go to the forest to beat up foreigners. I reposted it with a comment saying, 'This is unbelievable. How can this be happening in Poland, given our history.' Soon after, my old schoolfriend Marta texted me, telling me I should delete this post because I was giving these racists publicity. I replied, saying, 'Yes, good point, but I don't want to just sit here on my couch doing nothing when there is this crisis in the forest.' She texted me back: 'Do you have Signal?' I had no idea what that was. She told me to download the app and said she would come to my house the next day."

When Marta arrived the next morning, she explained that she was connected to a network of people helping migrants. She said six men from Senegal were hiding in the forest about two miles from Anna's house. For nearly two weeks, the group had been bringing the men food and clothing, but the men were stranded with nowhere to go, and their physical and mental health were deteriorating rapidly. They needed a place to stay while arrangements were made for their next move. Marta asked Anna if she could help.

Anna and her family had already decided that they wanted to do something. They had opened their home to strangers a few years earlier when they hosted a group of teenagers from Iran for a two-week cultural exchange, which went well.

"By October [2021], it was getting colder and more dangerous for people in the forest. I was thinking that I have a nice, big home, I have three cars, we have plenty of space. We don't have any close neighbors, so it would make a good safe house," Anna said.

But when Marta left the room, Anna's husband quietly voiced his concerns: "Okay, we want to help, but there will be six strangers, all men, in our home. We have two kids here. It's dangerous and irresponsible."

"We were up all night discussing this," Anna recalled to me. "I understood his fear. I told him, 'Look, darling, there is no family with blue eyes and blond hair in the forest. These are six men from Africa. We want to help, and this is how we can help. I don't think that people who are almost dying in the forest will be much danger to us.'"

By morning, her husband was on board and agreed to help.

Marta told Anna that she would organize everything through Signal. They would check if the road was safe from the border guards and bring the men the following night.

Anna's daughter, Zofia, who was fourteen years old at the time, said, "I was there when Marta came to our house and told us the plan. I had been at a sleepover with my friends, and when I came home, my mum told me the men would be arriving at our house that night. I was a little bit scared, to be honest, and asked if I could stay in my mum's room. I also knew that my parents could get in trouble with the police. But we had decided as a family. We all agreed that we would help. So I started to prepare dinner because we knew when they arrived, they would be hungry."

Zofia remembered that night well, how she watched the men from a window as they arrived. They walked past the outdoor firepit, which Zofia had always thought of as "a happy place full of good memories of family gatherings and parties." But that night, the men walking by looked like the walking dead, with gray skin and matted hair. Once inside the house, Zofia could see that they were terrified and ravaged by stress.

"They didn't even speak," Zofia recalled. "We said hello, and they nodded, but they didn't want to make a sound. They all went upstairs to take showers."

Although the family offered them the downstairs bathroom, they were too afraid to use it because of the window there and the risk of being seen. Zofia remembered the men's overwhelming fear in those first few hours in her home.

"They sat with us, and we started to eat, and there was just silence," said Zofia.

The next morning the men came down the stairs warily.

"We all started smiling a bit more," Zofia recalled, "and then laughing a little. They had spent two weeks terrified, but they were trying to make conversation, asking things like 'How is school?' I thought, 'What? You almost died yesterday; what do you mean, how is school?' Later that day, everyone began to relax. It was funny because they even organized shifts to clean the house, and it was clear that some of these grown men had no idea how to do that."

The arrival of the six men coincided with the garage roof repairs Anna had arranged a few weeks earlier.

"Normally when you have workmen, you bring them in for coffee, or give them breakfast; it's just good manners," she said. "But we told the workmen we had COVID and couldn't invite them in, and had to bring them coffee and cake outside. But from the top of the roof, they could see through a window into the house, so we covered that with a plastic bag."

Terrified of being seen, the refugees mostly stayed upstairs, keeping to themselves and watching nature documentaries on the Discovery Channel. They stayed for a week before being picked up and taken elsewhere by other volunteers. But they were just the first. Between October 2021 and May 2022, Anna's family secretly hosted thirty people, including children as young as five. The youngest to arrive unaccompanied was just thirteen. They were all from Africa or the Middle East.

One of them, Albert, remembered arriving at Anna's home in February 2022 after four days in the freezing forest: "There were four of us. We'd been surviving outdoors in minus-twenty-five

Celsius [minus-thirteen Fahrenheit temperatures]. We had sleeping bags, but it wasn't enough. One of us was so sick that we had to carry him around. Another lost his finger because of the cold. We were hungry and, honestly, losing hope."

Albert, who was in his early twenties at the time, came from a country in Africa that was torn by a civil war. In early 2022, he was studying in Russia. Fearing he would be returned to his home country when his visa expired, he decided to try to enter Europe via Belarus. He made it across the border into Poland but had been caught by border guards and forced back into Belarus. He decided to try again with three other guys.

"This was our last chance," said Albert. "We were getting desperate. Four days in the forest in that freezing cold is a long time. We finally contacted someone, and they brought us to Anna's house during the night."

Albert could hardly believe what he saw when they entered Anna's house.

"We were frozen. We walked in, and the whole family was there waiting for us," he recalled. "Wonderful people, just heartwarming. All I wanted was a place to put my head down and rest. So when I got to the house, I thought, 'I'm alive again.' We were from different countries and cultures, different beliefs, and you know, they put out all this food for us, halal food, just so thoughtful. I was surprised these good people trusted us. Total strangers. And how they would welcome us into their homes, into their families. They didn't know if we would be a potential threat or if they would be safe with us. I remember feeling as concerned about their safety as our own. They might have money or jewelry in the house, who knows, but when people show you trust, you don't betray them."

Many of those who spent weeks in the forest suffered from a range of medical issues, including infections and broken bones. Many required hospitalization. Egala, an organization providing humanitarian aid at the border, reported that one local hospital alone treated hundreds of people who had crossed the border—162 in 2023 and 258 in 2024.

Anna said that some of the people she hosted were unable to walk when they arrived. Exposure to freezing temperatures forces the body to shunt blood away from the limbs, a survival mechanism to protect vital organs, which can lead to numbness so severe that it can feel like paralysis. Thankfully, a volunteer doctor visited the house to give painkillers and special creams for damaged hands and feet and to take blood samples. Many migrants needed drugs for painful muscle cramps that were caused by exposure to the shivering cold for days and days.

To make matters far worse, in June 2022, Poland built a 120-mile-long, 5.5-yard-high fence topped with razor wire at the border to deter migrants, which led to an increase in broken bones and cuts to hands and arms as people climbed over it.

Since September 2021, at least ninety people have died attempting to cross into Poland from Belarus, according to the We Are Monitoring group, a Polish civil society organization. But NGOs say the real death toll is far greater.

"The situation was so crazy. I just believed someone would see sense and stop it. Meanwhile, I'm giving people food and shelter in my home—how is that bad?" said Anna. "I'm not religious, I don't pray, but for me, it was unbelievable that people were there in the forest. We are a Catholic country, we had a pope from Poland, and we were proud of all that, and I was raised in that spirit. And for me, if someone needs your help, you give it."

Even as a teenager, Anna had wanted to help people whom society prefers to ignore. When she was just thirteen, she wrote to a priest in Warsaw who was supporting people with drug addictions, offering to help.

"Yes, it was my teenage dream," she said, laughing. "At that time, the whole of society was against people who were addicted to drugs or who were infected with HIV. Some people wanted to kill them. It's the exact same story that's happening to immigrants now."

The priest wrote back to Anna, and they exchanged a few letters about his work and her interest in doing something useful.

"He was extraordinary, not like a normal priest," Anna said. "His mission was working with people with addictions, and he was open to helping everyone, whether they were trans or gay or whatever."

Anna had been too young to get involved then, but in high school, she joined a local group supporting people with drug problems.

"They were organizing a summer camp for kids from disadvantaged or difficult backgrounds, sometimes with parents who struggled with drugs or alcohol," recalled Anna. "So we took these kids for the whole summer to camps on the Baltic Sea. At first, I brought one school friend with me to help. By the final year of high school, out of thirty-two people in my class, twenty-eight of us were working at the camp."

Anna's generosity toward the migrants in need of help had a similar effect on those around her. Accustomed to Anna's ways of helping others, her family and friends supported her work in sheltering people by supplying food and raising money to get them clothes.

"Some people knew we were doing something, but not exactly what," said Anna. "I knew there were other safe houses, because those we hosted let slip about other places they'd stayed . . . it was better not to know for security."

Anna's home was one of the safe houses sheltering migrants that I visited when I was working with local activists. Tucked away in a quiet area with no immediate neighbors, it seemed to be the ideal place for people to stay after the horrors of the forest, to recuperate and brace themselves for the next stage of their journey. But even though the home felt remote, a nearby hotel regularly accommodated soldiers and police, putting the family and those they hosted in constant fear of being exposed.

"Dozens of army officers and policemen were stationed just five hundred yards away," Zofia said. "One day, I was standing in our kitchen with this Syrian guy named Ahmed, [who was] staying with us. We were preparing a meal, looking out of our big kitchen window, when we saw police cars passing by. Ahmed just froze. His face went white. We were so terrified, we just stood there in silence. But they just drove past our house to the hotel."

Anna wasn't just secretly hosting people. She was also joining other volunteers during the night, making dangerous and exhausting trips into the forest to bring supplies to people stranded there.

"It was physically hard," Anna noted. "I'm not that keen on sport, and there were times when we were literally running through the forest to hide from soldiers. It's dark, and sometimes there's snow, or you're running across a plowed field, and it's hard going. We were carrying heavy bags with water and food, and it was just exhausting. For young people, it was easier. And you know what? In my experience, nearly everyone who I saw helping in the forest was a woman. A few men, but nearly all women."

Anna was regularly stopped and harassed by soldiers, border guards, and masked local vigilantes on these visits into the forest, sometimes for hours at a time. At times, she was held at gunpoint, photographed, and intimidated before finally being allowed to continue.

"Once I was stopped when I was alone in my car, and six guys surrounded it and wouldn't let me go," she recalled.

Anna's experience was far from isolated. Since 2021, I have heard dozens of accounts from human rights activists on the border describing harassment and attacks, including by Polish authorities. Some activists working in the area have also faced judicial harassment, been charged with crimes such as people smuggling, and brought to trial. In September 2025, after a long trial and intense national scrutiny, five activists—known as the Hajnówka Five—were acquitted of charges of providing "illegal assistance" to refugees and facilitating their stay in Poland. The charges carried a sentence of up to five years in prison. In 2022, the group had helped an Iraqi family with seven children and an elderly Egyptian man stranded in the forest by providing them with food and clothing. They were driving the migrants to the nearest town when they were intercepted by border guards.

I knew one of the accused, a young man named Mariusz. We first met when we drove into Ukraine together in the weeks after Russia's full-scale invasion in 2022. He had passed his driving test only a few days earlier—and frankly, he probably shouldn't have. With Mariusz at the wheel, we careened from Poland into Ukraine under air raid alarms in a car crammed with flak jackets for medics and boxes of baby food. I gave evidence to the court about his good character, saying I knew him to be motivated by altruism and by his determination to help vulnerable people, often at personal cost. The verdict was seen as a major win for those helping migrants, but there have been other prosecutions of other activists doing similar things elsewhere in Europe.

In Latvia, for instance, human rights activist Ieva Raubiško was convicted of giving aid to Syrian asylum seekers stranded at the Belarusian border and sentenced to two hundred hours of community service. Although Polish courts have generally sided with activists, there is a widespread belief that there will be further cases brought, with activists citing the large numbers of people questioned by police in the past year.

"Maybe all activists are in danger, because who knows who has said what to the police," one woman who helps refugees told me.

Anna and Zofia could still be prosecuted if their identities were known, but Anna said she would go crazy if she stopped helping others.

"For us, sheltering people might mean a week or more of high stress, but for those people fleeing in the forest, their whole life can depend on what we do for them," Anna observed. "Imagine you're in your house and you know that, like, less than a mile away, there are people dying. Do you say to yourself, 'Okay, let's go to sleep, let's go to dinner while they die'? It's not normal. I still believe in some kind of sense of morality or justice, and despite everything, I still believe that Poland is not as bad as other places. It's not like hiding Jewish people during the Second World War. I'm not risking my life." Remarkably, Zofia never told any of her friends about the secret life at her home. She compartmentalized her life:

> I wanted to keep those worlds separate. When I got home from school some days, my mum would say, "In ten minutes, five boys from Africa will arrive." That somehow became normal home life, and it was intense, and all I heard at home was the forest this, the forest that, forest, forest. So at school, I wanted something else, a different life, where we would talk about parties or go and grab some food in the afternoons. Then I go home, and there are refugees hiding upstairs, then the next day, back to school with my friends. It was just smart to cut these things off from each other; that's how I dealt with it. One of our teachers said something once about the soldiers at the border and how great they were. Some classmates agreed with her, some didn't, but I just listened and didn't say anything.

It was a big secret for a fourteen-year-old to carry.

"It would have been good gossip to tell people," Zofia said, "but also a good way for my parents to end up in prison. So I never told anyone. Never."

Secrecy is often an inescapable part of activism. Not being able to confide in others about the pressure you are under brings enormous stress and, at times, a sense of isolation.

Many writers have described the tension of this "double life" of staying true to themselves in a world of disinformation and propaganda. As the German-American philosopher Hannah Arendt put it, "The ideal subject of totalitarian rule is not the convinced Nazi or the convinced Communist, but people for whom the distinction between fact and fiction . . . and the distinction between true and false . . . no longer exist." Accepting his 1970 Nobel Prize for Literature, Russian dissident Alexander Solzhenitsyn said, "The simple act of an ordinary brave man is not to participate in lies, not to support false actions!"

Anna never doubted they were doing the right thing, even with the risk of going to prison. She was simply following her personal truth.

"I believe we should try to behave normally," she said, "but what's happening is not normal. . . . If one day I go to court for what I did, I know I am still in line with what I think and I feel, and that is the most important thing for me."

Some people stayed at Anna's house for a couple of days, others for up to two weeks. They usually left on short notice.

Anna said, "We would get a call saying they would have to move that evening, or the next morning."

Albert, who arrived at Anna's home in February 2022 via Russia, recovered there for a week before moving on. He eventually made it to England, where he was granted legal status to stay. Albert now lives in the United Kingdom and has earned a scholarship to study neuroscience in London at one of the country's most prestigious universities—a future that once seemed impossible.

"I aim to be a neurosurgeon," he said. "People like Anna and her family helped me along my journey, and I want to help others in return."

By May 2022, the summer was returning, and those helping the people in the forest were better organized, so there was less need for the sort of emergency help provided by Anna's family. But they have continued to help those seeking official recognition as refugees.

Abdoulah, from West Africa, applied for asylum after crossing the border through the forest. In late 2022, he was waiting to learn whether he would be allowed to stay in Poland. When he found out his claim had been rejected, he suffered a seizure and was hospitalized for several weeks.

"The doctor said I could only leave the hospital if I had somewhere to live where I wouldn't be left on my own," he told me. "Anna took me in, and I stayed at her home for over two months. I felt like a member of the family. Everyone showed me love. I started to regain my spirits. Anna came with me to the border guards when I had to sign various documents and came with me on hospital visits. Slowly but surely, I got my confidence back."

Abdoulah now lives in France, where he was granted asylum.

Anna stays in regular contact with nearly all those she hosted. She and Zofia have visited some of them in countries across Europe where they have settled. While some are thriving, others struggle with the aftermath of trauma.

"One guy from Syria, twenty- or twenty-one years old, had seen all his family killed in front of him in the war. He was in a deep depression," said Anna. "I was in touch with people caring for him in Berlin for a while, but there wasn't much optimism about what was happening or what would happen to him."

Anna and Zofia are still processing the stress of the experience. Memory loss is a common symptom of trauma.

"We have black holes in our memory," said Anna. "There are details from those times we just can't remember."

In 2025, Poland suspended the right of migrants arriving via the border with Belarus to claim asylum—a move that proved popular with the public. Yet those desperate to escape danger continue to risk the forest crossing. The fear of what will happen to those who are helping people is increasing.

"I know that it's possible to go to jail for this," said Anna. "I am ready for that. I know it would be really very difficult for my children, for my family, for my friends. But if you ask me, would I change the past if it means going to jail? I wouldn't. There are some moments in your life when you have to choose."

CHAPTER 3

BÜLENT ŞIK, TURKEY

On the morning of February 7, 2019, scientist Bülent Şık stood in the dock at Istanbul's Çağlayan Palace of Justice, Europe's largest courthouse, and nervously began to read his statement. Charged with three crimes, including espionage, he knew that if found guilty, he could be convicted of terrorism and face up to twelve years in prison. He offered no alibi and made no claim of mistaken identity. Instead, he repeated, in even greater detail, the information that led to his prosecution in the first place—material he had already made public.

"When the trial started and it was my turn to take the floor, I read out the text of the speech I had prepared," he said. "The judge didn't seem to notice what I was doing. He didn't interrupt me. I read it out as if I were giving a lecture at university. The whole process I went through, the years-long research project about pollution causing cancer in children, from beginning to end, as if I were telling a story."

The dock was in many ways a strange place for Bülent to have found himself. Though he was an internationally respected food engineer, renowned for his meticulous research and thorough analysis, his journey to academia had been a long and challenging one.

"I didn't really grow up in a house full of books," he said. "My father was a truck driver, and my mother had only a primary school level education. We were not well off."

Bülent's uncle, a well-known attorney named Ahmet Albay, was the only one in his mother's family to receive a college education. He became a major influence on his nephew. Bülent said that from the age of around twelve, he began spending the summers hanging around his uncle's law offices.

"There were always all sorts of interesting people passing through to see him," recalled Bülent. "And he was always recommending things for me to read. I wanted to read whatever I could lay my hands on. I got books from school. My mother even arranged for me to go to the local library. By the time I was a young teen, I'd read a lot of the classics—Turkish writers, but other things, too. Jack London was one of my favorites."

Uncle Ahmet soon gained notoriety as one of three attorneys representing the survivors and bereaved family members of the 1978 Maraş Massacre, in which more than a hundred people were murdered, and more than a thousand injured, by far-right extremists in Kahramanmaraş, a historic southern Turkish city. The case inflamed passions across the country, and Bülent's uncle knew it was dangerous to take it on.

"I remember asking him why he didn't accept the police protection he was entitled to," said Bülent. "He told me that he didn't want to risk anyone else's life protecting him."

In 1980, when Bülent was fourteen, his uncle was assassinated because of his work on the Maraş Massacre case. He was shot in the back by a member of a fascist group while he was getting into his car. He lay in a coma for sixteen days before passing away. He was just thirty-seven years old. The murder darkened an already challenging adolescence for Bülent, which also included seeing many of his neighbors and friends arrested in the poor district of Adana, the city in southern Turkey where he grew up.

That same year Turkey itself teetered on the brink of crisis. The streets were torn by clashes between leftist and rightist groups, the economy was in turmoil, and a succession of hastily assembled governments kept collapsing. In September 1980, the military staged a coup, claiming it was the only way to restore order. The generals imposed martial law, dissolved parliament, and banned political parties. More than half a million people were detained, and widespread torture and executions marked a new level of state repression. In Bülent's neighborhood, hundreds of residents were detained, including both of his parents.

"My mother witnessed things in police custody—abuse and torture that sent her into a deep depression," he recalled. "My early impressions of political power were about oppression. And violence."

Bülent's teenage dreams of one day becoming a lawyer like his uncle now looked distant, but a high-school chemistry teacher who saw his potential encouraged him to consider college.

"He persuaded me to apply for the science stream at university," Bülent said. "The grades required for the science courses were so high, I feared I wouldn't make them, but I thought I might get good enough grades to study law instead."

Much to his surprise, Bülent's exam results qualified him for the science subjects, and he was also given a job as an undergraduate working in a government lab at the Ministry of Agriculture and Fisheries. But he still wanted to be a lawyer, so he spent a year studying with the law faculty, too.

"I realized the work as a food engineer was much more interesting than I thought it would be, so I gave up the law," said Bülent.

When he finished his degree, his professors insisted he stay on to do a master's, but financial pressures at home meant he had to go to work full-time, and he didn't get back to the university for seven years.

Meanwhile, Bülent's interest in food safety and environmental pollution continued to grow. In his spare time, he immersed himself in academic papers, studies, and research on the subject.

"I can't really explain why I was so drawn to it," he said, "but I soon realized that toxins in food weren't just a technical matter—they were a social and public health issue."

His growing obsession with food safety even became a running joke among his friends, who watched him scrutinize the labels on every product he bought.

He would spend nineteen years working on food safety research in government labs before starting his doctorate at the age of thirty-eight. At the unusually late age of forty-two, he became a university professor and helped set up a food analysis lab at a university in Antalya, in southwestern Turkey.

"We were researching toxins in food and their effect on children," he recalled. "I was always interested in how this environmental pollution damages children's health. I wrote one study in 2012 and sent out a press release outlining the findings, and next thing I knew, a senior government bureaucrat called me and told me to retract it because it was seen as critical of the authorities. I refused, but I was shocked. It was a wake-up call. It shattered this idealistic image I had of academia and of academic independence."

Around that time, work had begun on a major government research project that would evaluate how environmental factors influence the cancer rate in the industrialized areas of northwest Turkey. The Ministry of Health coordinated the project, which involved dozens of academics from various departments of eleven universities. It was already known that cancer rates in Turkey were much higher in some parts of the country than others, and the government commissioned the research to identify carcinogenic (cancer-causing) chemicals in the environment in Kocaeli Province, which reported the highest number of cancer cases in Turkey, and in the Edirne, Kırklareli, and Tekirdağ Provinces in the Ergene River Basin as well.

According to the World Health Organization (WHO), cancer causes one in six deaths worldwide, about 16 percent of all causes of death. Turkey generally has a better record than this average, with cancer causing one in every eight deaths (13 percent). In Antalya, where heavy industry is limited, the situation is even better, with only one in ten deaths caused by cancer. But the rates in Turkey's industrialized regions are alarmingly high. In Tekirdağ, Kırklareli, and Edirne, cancer accounts for one in four deaths.

These regions host a wide range of industries, including chemical plants, steel mills, textile factories, and food processing, all of which contribute to air, water, and soil pollution. The study aimed to trace the relationship between pollution in some provinces and the general health of people living there. It was one of the largest public health studies ever conducted, examining conditions of millions of people across a huge area.

When it began, Bülent wasn't playing a central role, but that changed quickly.

"When I suggested a methodology to collect the data to make the analysis easier, I was invited into the senior research team," Bülent said. "This was a really exciting prospect, being part of a study with huge resources and with the prospect of really making a difference to people's health."

Bülent was enthusiastic about the chance to analyze such a large data set. Hundreds of experienced scientists collected the data. He collected some of it himself as well, but mostly focused on the analysis. The idea was to assess all the data together and create a map of where the highest cancer risks were found.

"There are obviously close links between various diseases and our environment. If smoking is excluded, many diseases, especially cancer, are linked more to the environment than to our individual choices and habits. This isn't just true of cancer, but of many other health problems, too," he said.

The main focus of the research, Bülent explained, concerned children's health:

> Many toxic chemicals cause various health problems, including infertility, reproductive health disorders, hormonal and nervous system disorders, obesity, respiratory diseases, and liver and kidney failure. The most critical point here is age. The younger the age, the greater the risk to health. Children are much more sensitive to toxic chemicals than adults. The ways toxic substances enter the body, and the amount of exposure, are important. Generally, the harmful effects increase as the dose increases, although there are some exceptions. For example, toxic chemicals that disrupt hormonal systems and nervous systems can be harmful at even very low doses. The toxins cause the most harm to infants and children, especially those below the age of fourteen.

International academic studies show an increase in childhood cancers worldwide, the highest rates among those living in chemically polluted environments. Around 7 percent of cancers are strictly hereditary, the other 93 percent caused by genetics interacting with the environment. Children are most at risk from environmental pollution.

"In this research commissioned by the Ministry of Health, we investigated the residues of many toxic chemicals in food and water that harm reproductive, hormonal, and neurological systems in children," Bülent explained. "We found residues of various toxic substances, such as heavy metals, pesticides, and harmful polyaromatic compounds, which were having very damaging effects on children's health."

There are approximately one million children aged seventeen or younger in the provinces of Tekirdağ, Kirklareli, Edirne, and Kocaeli, where much of the research was focused.

One of the substances tested for was lead. According to the WHO, lead is among the ten toxic substances posing the greatest risk to public health, particularly because of its harmful effects on young children.

"Exposure to lead in childhood—the first six years, including the period in the womb, are critical—causes damage to the brain and nervous system, slows growth, causes anemia, hearing loss, and behavioral and learning problems," Bülent explained. "In adults, lead exposure causes hypertension, impaired kidney function, and impaired fertility. There is no established exposure level or limit value for lead in children. In other words, every dose of lead exposure is toxic to children; ideally, children should not be exposed to lead at all. The more we can protect them from lead exposure, the better."

Thousands of samples were taken from villages, neighborhoods, and people living in various settlements in the Ergene Basin and Kocaeli regions to investigate the chemicals that cause different cancers. Ground and surface water, soil, air, and food samples from the region were analyzed for carcinogenic chemical residues. The results were compared with the findings in Antalya Province, where there were no industrial activities, to see the difference.

The research was divided into sixteen different topics and focused on the quality of the air people breathe, as well as what they eat and drink. Bülent's particular expertise was on possible contamination in water and food. As the data from the field research was coming in, Bülent quickly realized the situation was far worse than anticipated.

"We found widespread lead contamination in the drinking water in these three provinces, [Tekirdag, Kirklareli, Edirne] even though it was below the limit allowed by Turkish law," he said.

"The study showed that the drinking water in 52 out of 764 neighborhoods in those provinces was contaminated with lead and other heavy metals."

While none of the samples from the nonindustrialized Antalya Province exceeded the limit set for lead, two of the samples from Kocaeli Province and four of the samples from the Ergene Basin provinces were above the limit, meaning those waters should never be used as drinking water.

The scientists also looked at levels of arsenic and aluminum in the water of the industrialized areas, comparing them to levels in nonindustrialized Antalya and to international limits that are considered safe.

Arsenic was found in more than 40 percent of samples from the industrialized areas at levels fifteen times higher than in Antalya. Levels above the limit were detected in more than 3 percent of the samples, which means that the water should not be used as drinking water.

The WHO limits the maximum amount of aluminum in water at two hundred micrograms per liter. Drinking water with levels above this limit is a health hazard, and prolonged exposure, depending on the severity, can lead to neurological, kidney, and bone health problems. The samples showed that aluminum levels in the water in Ergene were very high, with 3.8 percent of the samples above the two-hundred-microgram limit. In Kocaeli Province, more than 9 percent of the samples were above the limit. The results clearly showed it was not safe for residents to drink the water. By comparison, the levels of aluminum detected in Antalya were generally very low.

Bülent also noted that foods may contain pesticides at levels considered acceptable. However, when several different pesticides are present—even if each one is below its individual limit—their combined effect can still cause serious harm. Bülent said one of the most striking findings from the research was that more than half of the food samples from industrialized regions contained residues from multiple pesticides.

At the end of 2015, the fieldwork was completed, and the research came to an end. The study results were overlaid on a map of Turkey to see whether carcinogenic-chemical pollution was concentrated in the areas with the highest incidence of cancer. In a December 2015 meeting, all the academics involved shared their findings. The results were highly alarming.

"I knew the data looked bad as I was analyzing it, but when everyone else shared theirs, it was obvious there was a major problem," Bülent said.

Government officials were present at the December meeting. The scientists asked what actions the government planned to take in response to the findings.

"They gave a very careful, political answer, saying they would take it to the [Health] minister and follow his instructions. That's when I first felt uneasy about how the government might respond," Bülent said. "But it was such a large project, and so many people knew the results, I didn't think they could possibly cover it up."

As Bülent waited for the Ministry of Health to publish the findings, Turkish security forces were intensifying their campaign against the militant Kurdistan Workers' Party (PKK) in the southeast of the country. The renewed violence came after the collapse of a two-year ceasefire between the government and the PKK, ending hopes of a peaceful resolution to a conflict that has claimed more than forty thousand lives since the 1980s. Following the breakdown of a ceasefire in July 2015, entire towns were sealed off under curfew as soldiers moved in, and civilians were caught in the crossfire of a conflict that felt never-ending.

Bülent was one of about 1,100 academics from eighty-nine universities in Turkey who signed a petition, known as "Academics for Peace," stating, "We will not be a party to this crime!" and calling on the government to end the crackdown and start peace negotiations.

The petition was made public on January 11, 2016. Turkish President Recep Tayyip Erdoğan immediately labeled the signatories "so-called intellectuals" and accused them of treason. All signatories were targeted, and many were arrested. Government supporters appeared on television to condemn the academics, calling them terrorists and threatening them with violence.

"To be honest, no one expected such a harsh and angry reaction from the government," Bülent said. "They said things publicly like 'We will wash ourselves in your blood, because you are traitors.' It was a very difficult time."

Six months later, the government crackdown intensified following an attempted coup by a faction within the Turkish military. On the night of Friday, July 15, 2016, a group of officers tried to overthrow the government, seizing key military sites and blocking bridges in Istanbul. Fighter jets bombed the parliament building in Ankara, and the chief of the General Staff was taken hostage by the coup plotters. Within hours, however, military units loyal to President Erdoğan, supported by police and civilians, rallied and fought back. The coup attempt had effectively collapsed by dawn, only hours after it had begun.

At least 250 people were killed and thousands injured in the attempted coup. In its aftermath, security forces launched a sweeping crackdown, and a two-year state of emergency was declared. Thousands were soon arrested, and more than 125,000 public employees—including judges, soldiers, teachers, and academics—were dismissed or suspended.

"The government used the failed coup to get rid of the scientists who do not hesitate to oppose the government, who do science with a public understanding, with an eye to the social good and the welfare of the people. They wanted to replace us with their own people," said Bülent.

By November 2016, Bülent was one of several academics fired from their jobs at his university. By 2017, he had been declared persona non grata by the authorities, and his communication with officials at the Health Ministry was cut off, leaving him with no way of knowing when the government might release the results or whether any plans existed for making them public. Bülent asked a friend who was a doctor and a Member of Parliament to ask the government when the results of the studies would be released. Two weeks later, his friend came back and said the ministry claimed no such project existed.

"I thought it was impossible that something so big, involving so many academics, could be kept secret—but it had," said Bülent. "That was the moment I realized that they weren't going to release the results of the study. Instead, they were going to bury them."

He decided that the only thing he could do was to review the remaining data from the study himself.

"I had taken a file copy of the analyses home from my office computer as a backup. Thank God I still had my personal computer with me when I left the university. So I started going through the data to figure out in which areas these high levels of carcinogenic pollutants were. It took me a year of work to figure out what was going on."

Bülent said that what was particularly difficult was analyzing the data on his own. He was ostracized by other scientists who had worked on the project, who were afraid to be seen with him.

"People stayed away from me," he said. "Some were close friends. And the hardest thing was not being sure if I had analyzed everything correctly because I had no one to consult with. Nobody wanted to hear from me because I was labeled a terrorist, a 'peace academic.' I was alone."

He struggled on, meticulously analyzing all the data he had, determined not to make a mistake. He checked and rechecked and rechecked the data.

"I wanted to know what it all meant," he said, "where this pollution threat was most serious, because people have to know—people have to know what they eat, what they drink, what they breathe."

When Bülent was sure of the findings, he decided to publish the results.

"I did not hesitate," he said simply. "It felt right to make it public. The people who lived in those places had a right to know what the study was saying. I've always seen it as a public health issue—I've tried to depoliticize it and talk about it in the context of the danger to people's safety, and especially the health of children."

Not one of the other researchers openly supported him.

"One of the senior academics in the study even phoned me and warned me not to make the findings public, saying it would cause me problems, and telling me to stop it," Bülent said. "Wow, I had this naive idea that some scientists from other parts of the study would come out and talk about the other results, but nobody did."

An influential newspaper called the *Cumhuriyet* ("The Republic") agreed to publish the findings. Widely considered the last remaining opposition newspaper in Turkey, with its strong tradition of investigating state secrecy, the outlet was a natural refuge for Bülent's work. (Journalists in Turkey operate in a highly repressive environment; the country ranks 159 out of 180 on the 2025 World Press Freedom Index compiled by Reporters Without Borders.) The revelations ran in a series of articles over four days beginning on April 15, 2018, under the headline "The State Hid the Products That Gave Turkey Cancer, We Reveal Them! Here Is the Poison List."

On the second day of the series' publication, the Health Ministry filed a criminal complaint against Bülent for "causing public outrage" and "affecting foreign purchases." He was charged with "disclosing prohibited confidential information, obtaining prohibited confidential information," and "disclosing secrets related to his duty."

"I knew it would cause me trouble," Bülent said. "I knew I would be vilified, but I had to do it. But I was accused of much more than I'd anticipated. I didn't expect espionage charges."

Undaunted, he used the time between the indictment in July 2018 and the opening court date in February 2019 to work more intensively on the research.

"It was a tough time because my father died a month before the first court date. I had to focus and stay positive. I knew that the first session of the trial would be very important, that it would be a chance to explain more data not included in the newspaper articles."

As the trial date neared and word of the case spread, Bülent began to receive a lot of support, especially from the legal community.

"Eleven representatives of the major law associations in Turkey backed me, and they managed to get the court venue changed to the Justice Palace," he said. "That was important because it had the facilities to record the proceedings electronically, so I knew my words couldn't be summarized, edited, or censored."

That's how Bülent Şık came to be in the dock that February morning in 2019, softly delivering his statement as though he was giving a university lecture.

"In that first hearing, I wanted to respond to the accusations, and I decided to explain the details of the study—in particular, the name of each project, the registration number in the official documents, and what was done during the project work. Simply disclosing the titles of the projects would mean a lot to interested scientists and, of course, to the public. I had not been able to include these details in my articles in the newspaper. But this meant doing what I had already been accused of in the courtroom: continuing to disclose information about the project. My lawyer friends rightly expressed their concerns about the wisdom of doing this."

Speaking from the dock, he began: "In order to respond to the accusations in the indictment against me, I would like to briefly outline the purpose and scope of the project carried out by the Turkish Ministry of Health. . . ." From there, he carried on, reading out twelve pages of the statement.

"When I'd finished reading it out, my lawyers gave me a thumbs-up, and honestly, I left the court that day with a sense of victory," Bülent said. "I'd had my say, and there were a lot of reporters there who heard the truth."

Bülent used each of his three court appearances that year—in February, May, and September—to talk about the research and the responsibility of scientists to stand with humanity and protect people's rights. He recalled that at the third hearing, as the judge delivered the verdict, he sounded astonished and said, "You show no sign of remorse."

In the courtroom that day, Bülent explained his courageous stance: "Living in a chemically polluted environment is a problem that cannot be overcome by changing our individual preferences and habits. Preventing the destruction of the natural environment is a key strategy in the fight against cancer. It is as much a necessity for a citizen to support struggles against environmental pollution as it is for public institutions to prevent environmental pollution."

He also elaborated on his duties as an academic, asserting, "A scientist cannot and should not stay away from the struggles carried out on this issue. On the contrary, he/she should see it as a fundamental responsibility to carry his/her knowledge and the results of his/her studies to the public sphere, to create public debates, to inflame the public debates on this issue, and to take part in these debates, not on the sidelines. Institutions may remain silent in the face of social problems, but a scientist should not."

The court ruled on the three charges against Bülent. While he was acquitted of obtaining prohibited information and disclosing prohibited information, he was found guilty of disclosing confidential information and sentenced to fifteen months in prison. His sentence was not suspended because, as the judge had noted, he showed no remorse for his actions.

Weeks later, six hundred academics from around the world, including Judith Butler and Roald Hoffmann, signed a petition calling on the court to nullify its decision. Paris-based NGO Reporters Without Borders said that the conviction was a "profoundly unjust act of censorship."

Bülent appealed the court's decision and was allowed to remain free while the appeal process continued. The case dragged on in various courts for six years until he was finally acquitted in April 2025 by the 13th Criminal Chamber of the Istanbul Regional Court of Appeals.

"At the beginning I was sure I would be sentenced to twelve years in prison, but in the end there was such support from the international community—academics and others—and such pressure on the court that I thought a lighter sentence would be given," Bülent said. "My lawyers had my opening statement translated into English and sent it out internationally. It was taken up by the Collegium Ramazzini, Scholars at Risk, the Union of Concerned Scientists, Article 19, Amnesty International, the National Academy of Sciences in the US, and other international bodies. This support really helped get the espionage charge dropped."

Bülent insisted that what he did was not an act of bravery.

"This wasn't about courage but about scientific responsibility," he said.

When the government filed a lawsuit against him, Bülent and a group of academics, journalists, and supporters discussed how best to defend themselves and explain the situation to the public. Some argued that, at its core, the case was about freedom of speech, that an academic warning the public about health risks should not be treated as a criminal. Bülent didn't disagree, but further argued that "the essence of the case is protecting children's health," and so when they publicized the court case on social media, the issue they stressed was children's health above all else.

Despite finally being found innocent of all charges, Bülent was unable to return to his job at the university.

"I am now officially retired with a small pension," he said.

He is struggling to find another job, but is certain that what he did was right.

"The most important thing for me was the exposure of children to these carcinogens," he said. "I wanted everyone who has children to be aware of the dangers of what they breathe, eat, and drink."

A decade after the data was first presented to the Health Ministry, the Turkish government has apparently taken no action, claiming it is still analyzing the results. In fact, Bülent says that since the research was conducted, pollution has worsened dramatically, with toxins now spreading from the rivers into the sea and with new gold and coal mines only adding to the contamination.

Despite losing the university position he had worked for many years to attain, Bülent is now recognized worldwide for his scientific integrity and achievements. He continues to track water pollution, collect data, and warn communities about the risks to children.

CHAPTER 4

JOHANNA NEJEDLOVÁ, CZECH REPUBLIC

Wednesday night, December 9, 2015, was a typically cold evening in the Czech capital of Prague. When twenty-five-year-old Johanna Nejedlová got home from her busy job at a travel agency, she turned on her computer and scrolled idly through Facebook. One post quickly jolted her. Sixty-three percent of people in the Czech Republic, men and women, thought a woman was at least partly responsible if she was raped, according to a survey by Amnesty International. Johanna told me the comments below the post made her "super angry, because they were just confirming the view that rape is somehow a woman's fault."

In the Czech Republic, a central European country of ten million, official statistics barely reveal the extent of sexual violence. About seven hundred cases of rape are reported to the police each year. But according to Amnesty International, the real number is in the thousands, as many victims are afraid to speak out due to shame, fear, and cruel stigma. NGOs have noted that immigrant communities in particular stay silent for fear of losing their residency status.

Sitting at her computer that night, Johanna acted on impulse. Without thinking what she was doing, she wrote a Facebook post about her own experience, which began as follows:

> I just got pissed off at the discussion under the article about rape. I haven't talked about it for a long time. . . . It happened to me a while ago. I thought it needed to be talked about. So that people would know that it happens to girls, you know. But instead of people sympathizing, they said it was my own fault, that I should watch how I dress. They said I'm a pretty girl, I must take care of myself, and I can't go out alone without a male companion. If there's booze involved, then whatever happens may well be my fault. If no one is holding a knife to your throat and if no blood is drawn, it's not rape.
>
> A lot of people around me don't talk about it. They had bad luck with a taxi driver, with a guy they had been dating for a long time and were just breaking up with, with a friend, with a friend's boyfriend.

The problem Johanna described goes far beyond the Czech Republic. The UN estimates that one in three women around the world has experienced physical and/or sexual abuse, mostly by intimate partners, and it continues to be "vastly underreported."

At the end of her 560-word post, Johanna pointed out that the United States had an organization called Men Can Stop Rape (now known as MCSR), which promotes healthy models of masculinity through education. She asked, "Is there not something like that in the Czech Republic? And if not, is there anyone among you who would like to start organizing something like that?"

Johanna had accidentally set her post to "public" rather than limiting it to her friends. Though she had meant for her questions to be rhetorical, impassioned messages from people keen to get involved filled her inbox overnight. The response left her astonished.

"I thought . . . 'Fuck, now I should meet with them or something,'" she said.

When I was working for Amnesty International in the early 2000s, the organization began commissioning surveys on attitudes toward sexual violence around the world. I still remember the 2005 survey on British people's views, because it caused widespread debate in the media. The findings were shocking: One-fifth of the populace said a woman was partly at fault if she wore "revealing clothing" or was drunk, and 96 percent didn't know the appalling incidence of rape around the UK. The surveys in Britain and elsewhere revealed an often hidden and very ugly truth, but one that needed to be made public if things were to improve.

Part of my work at Amnesty in those days was to locate interesting and effective activism being done by various Amnesty offices and supporters across the world, and to publicize and share those ideas with other sections. In the years that followed, several countries took up my suggestions, including the Czech Republic, in 2015.

Czech Amnesty was doing important work, but there was still a great deal of room for more activism. I didn't realize it at the time, but only a short walk from Amnesty's office in Prague, something new was quietly taking shape in the back room of a pub.

Sure enough, Johanna had arranged a meeting in that pub in response to the many messages she had received from her viral Facebook post. As such initial gatherings tend to be, it was a little chaotic. A few dozen people showed up—mostly women but some men, too—all eager to meet the woman behind the Facebook post. Johanna had no idea what to expect.

I met Johanna in a coffee shop in Prague's Old Town in September 2025. Though she texted me to say she was running a few minutes late, she arrived right on time and, adjusting her glasses, quickly ordered her favorite meal.

Johanna told me she didn't have a background in activism. Her mother, from the Czech Republic, and her father, from Chad, are both academics. But she admits to having a rebellious streak from a young age.

"I was the sort of kid who didn't follow the rules much, and I was pretty adventurous," she said. "I had an outdoors kind of life, hanging out with neighbors outside, climbing trees, running around. My mum would wave us off in the morning and say don't come back until lunchtime, that sort of thing."

When she was five, she moved with her mother and baby brother to the suburbs of Prague from the north of the country.

At school, she said, "teachers liked me even if I wasn't always very polite." She was "always a feminist, though I suppose I didn't call it that. I mean, as a kid, I didn't think it was fair that I was the one who was supposed to have a clean room and my brother didn't. And I never had a clean room."

She went to a small Jewish high school in Prague, and when she was around seventeen years old, she was part of a group that partied and drank.

"We were very hard to handle," she said.

After high school, she went straight to university to study Judaism and comparative religion. But she soon lost interest, dropped out, and started at the University of Agriculture, studying irrigation.

"That was definitely not for me," she laughed. "I think I knew that after a few days."

Johanna looked back on that first pub meeting in 2015—and on her entry into the world of activism a decade ago—with fondness and humor, often laughing at how little she knew back then.

"There was a lot of heated discussion. . . . We had very different ideas. Some wanted to organize self-defense training for girls, which wasn't something I was very interested in," she said. "There was another woman there—called Kateřina Kilianova—and we just clicked and started to organize more together."

Johanna and Kateřina came up with a lot of campaign ideas, but they didn't want to start their own organization.

"At first, we thought we'd hand over our work and ideas to another organization, one already working on this sort of thing," Johanna recalled.

But there were no takers, so they decided to try starting something on their own.

"We thought we'd register ourselves as an NGO, write some grant proposals, and get like $50,000 immediately," she said with a laugh.

The reality for grassroots organizations is much harsher. Funding is fiercely competitive, donors tend to favor established organizations, and building credibility can take years.

"We started to write totally useless proposals, actually very horrible. And it wasn't working at all," Johanna said. "It's hard to get money if you are just starting, and we had no story behind us, no track record, no experience."

Then, at exactly the right time, Johanna met by chance one of many people who would help her in the years to come. An American woman living in Prague, who worked with survivors of trauma, told her and Kateřina about small grants given by the local US embassy, specifically for women's rights issues.

"She helped us write the proposal, and somehow we got lucky, because they gave us $10,000—our first funds," said Johanna.

They were up and running.

Johanna and two other women she was working with had a lot of ideas about how to use the $10,000. In a way, their inexperience gave their imagination free rein.

"Not knowing much was somehow really useful. I had no idea of limits or how hard this was all going to be," she said.

As soon as they secured the funds, helping hands began cropping up from all quarters. Artists created an exhibition and online cartoon graphics. Gradually, a team of volunteers offering different skills came together, designing and building campaigns, all aiming to educate the public about consent and to dispel myths about rape.

Johanna explained what came to be known as "The Hindsight Fallacy": "If I were in a bar today, wearing a short skirt, getting drunk, and nothing happened to me, no one would say I did anything wrong. But if something did happen to me, if I was assaulted, they would find reasons for it, they would blame me, because they need to rationalize it."

At the time, Johanna said, existing initiatives focused mainly on supporting victims of sexual violence, mostly women. But her work since those early days of activism has been dedicated to prevention and raising awareness about issues of sexual violence while "explaining the causes and roots of it," she said. "Because of this, our narratives were different. Our focus has been less on the victims and more on talking about the perpetrators." Their campaign messages have included "Respect Is Sexy" and "When They Don't Want It, They Don't Want It."

One early impactful campaign was a short film produced with the help of an aspiring filmmaker Johanna had previously worked with in a bar.

"She was just starting out, trying to make films. So we did a storyboard, and she got some young people involved," Johanna said.

The film shows a man talking to his friend about a date with his girlfriend that didn't end well. He admits he continued having sex with her even though she didn't want to, and he attempts to justify it. His friend sets him straight, telling him sex without consent is "never okay."

Johanna said, "We were trying to show what sexual violence can look like. . . . Most people think of rape as a situation where you get mugged in a park, but it's not." She rightly pointed out that the majority of rapes worldwide are committed by someone the victim knew and often by a partner.

The next step was to get the advertisement in front of a large audience. It would have been easy to assume cinemas would refuse to show a video about rape, but Johanna and the volunteers, undeterred, gave it a shot.

"Amazingly, some cinemas did show it, even the big multiplexes," she said.

Not long after, the group held its first press conference with the help of another friend, a journalist.

"I'd never done anything like that before," Johanna said. "We were also sort of lucky with the timing—this was an issue that was somehow hanging in the air, and no one was really talking about it the way we were."

It seemed, though, the more their campaigns succeeded, the more vicious the online abuse on social media became.

"There were a lot of comments criticizing us. . . . It wasn't great, but it seemed sort of distant, far away," Johanna said. "Once, even my brother wrote in all caps on my Facebook page that we are all crazy, that what we're saying is impossible, asking why we hate all men. But that was at the start. He's very supportive now."

The emails and the messages sent to her phone were much more worrying.

"It was very, very scary. . . . They were invading my personal space. I got others, really ugly ones, and I even reported one of these to the police, but they weren't very helpful. I was often targeted because I stood out. It's easy to remember me. There aren't many other black people here," she said.

But she and a few other volunteers pushed on.

In October 2016, less than a year after her fateful first social media post, Johanna and two fellow activists set up the NGO Konsent. They could have hardly known that the entire world was on the brink of a reckoning. The following October, millions of women across the globe joined the Me Too movement, sharing their experiences of sexual harassment and abuse on social media.

Johanna observed that in the Czech Republic, Me Too "wasn't accepted very well at first." Although the movement helped raise Konsent's profile and drew more media attention to the NGO, they still faced a major challenge: Many people were not yet ready to speak openly about sexual violence.

"We were so naive at the start," said Johanna. "We were thinking, 'Yeah, soon everyone will know about this issue, and the problem will be solved, our work will be done.'"

But at first, only a few people went public with their stories because, Johanna explained, the country simply had no history of talking openly about this issue. The media also rarely addressed sexual violence, a consequence of men dominating editorial leadership in the news media—but that, she said, has begun to change.

Though their first year of campaigning was successful in reaching wide audiences, Johanna felt she wasn't getting to the root of the problem. That was when she and her colleagues decided to focus on teenagers.

"The best, most efficient thing was to talk about these issues before views are fixed. Changing an older person's mind is usually harder. No one wants to give up a long-held view," she said.

Recalling that the sex education offered at schools wasn't great, Johanna said, "All I was told was how to put on a condom, and we found that much of the advice about rape and consent being given to teenagers was basically telling girls to be careful, or some policeman would give talks to a class warning the girls not to stay out late."

Lacking the funds and expertise, Konsent crowdfunded a workshop on how to talk to young people about consent. The group soon found itself in the back of another pub, this time in Brno, about 200 kilometers [125 miles] from Prague. Fifteen people attended.

"Luckily, one [of them] knew something about education," Johanna said.

After several workshops, Johanna and her colleagues came up with effective lesson plans, but they weren't sure how to get them into classrooms.

"We thought we'd just email schools, and they'd say, 'Yeah, great, come in.' Turns out it doesn't work like that." She laughed.

Once again, the right people came through at the right time. Officials in the Department of Gender Equality had heard about Konsent's work and helped open doors to schools.

"That endorsement really mattered," said Johanna. "Having a government stamp of approval meant we weren't going to be blocked."

Having learned how to navigate institutions, Konsent realized it could take on an even bigger challenge—changing the country's laws. After years of public protests, in 2023, Konsent, together with Czech Amnesty, pressured the government to propose a new legal definition of rape to better protect victims. The new law, enacted in 2025, follows the "no means no" principle, in which physical or verbal coercion doesn't have to be proven, and a lack of consent can be shown by means other than verbal. In recent years, twelve other European countries have adopted consent-based laws, including Germany, Poland, the Netherlands, and Spain.

"From now on," Johanna said, "victims will have better representation in court and a better chance of a just punishment for the perpetrator."

Konsent's success has not come without huge difficulties, not least because of drastic funding cuts to NGOs that began in the United States and Europe in late 2024.

"In 2024, we were a team of fifteen," she said. "A year later, we were down to five. It's hard."

Like many activists around the world, Johanna and the Konsent team are having to get creative to raise income. Instead of relying on grants, the NGO now focuses on donations from the public via social media and fundraising drives by phone. Supporters even donate items that Konsent sells, from cinema tickets to boxes of condoms.

Konsent also successfully crowdfunded to produce a book for parents on how to talk to children about sex and consent.

"We sold over ten thousand copies in Czech bookshops," said Johanna. "Now it's in Polish and Slovakian, too. So that was a big help, though sales have probably peaked now."

Another challenge has been engaging men and preventing online radicalization. Again, this problem is not confined to the Czech Republic. Far from it. Younger men across the world, from the United States and the UK to Poland to South Korea, are increasingly voting for far-right groups. Online, men are turning to extreme communities within the "Manosphere," forums that promote misogyny and controversial ideas about masculinity.

"There are some really bad role models for men out there," Johanna said.

Konsent has recently been studying why men are drawn to the Manosphere. In response to what it has learned, the organization has distributed a booklet for educators, offering guidance on how to support boys emotionally and promote gender equality in schools. It is also collaborating with male influencers to spread healthier ideas about masculinity and hopes to secure funding to expand its work in schools.

"We're still at the beginning of this journey," Johanna said.

Even so, what she sparked from that Facebook post has helped transform the way the Czech Republic talks about sexual violence. Attitudes toward victims of rape have undoubtedly improved. In 2022, two-fifths (40 percent) of Czechs believed that victims may be partly to blame for the crime, lower than the three-fifths (60 percent) of Czechs in 2015.

Johanna was confident that even more progress had been made since 2022. "I think the numbers would be lower now," she said.

"Things are heading in the right direction. I am sure we helped a lot, but it's not just us."

Undoubtedly, Konsent has set an example to others. Similar organizations and groups around the world, including from Georgia, Ukraine, Britain, and India, have sought its advice.

Johanna's work with Konsent has received various awards, including the Woman in Youth Activism prize at the 2019 Women of Europe Awards, shortlisted alongside Swedish environmental activist Greta Thunberg. In 2020, Johanna was included in the Czech Forbes 30 under 30 for social enterprise.

Johanna has also ventured into politics, standing as a candidate for the European Parliament elections for the Green Party in 2024.

"I learned a lot during that campaign," she said. "It was all useful experience."

She still has plenty more work to do as an activist, including lobbying for the Czech government to ratify the Istanbul Convention, a Council of Europe agreement on preventing violence against women, which she has called a priority. Thirty-nine European countries have ratified the 2011 treaty, which requires governments to legislate against and prosecute gender-based violence. Amnesty International calls it "the gold standard" that can "save the lives of millions of women and girls."

"The convention should help to make sure there is sufficient care for victims of domestic and sexual violence," said Johanna, noting that it requires every regional city to have one center for victims of sexual violence. "Here, people would receive all the care they need—there would be a doctor, a police presence, and quality psychological and social assistance. . . . So far, we only have one such center, a completely new one, in Prague. I really believe that the state should be doing more work [to prevent sexual violence]. All our steps are about pushing the state to act."

Johanna is still learning, but she has come to realize that it doesn't take any special qualifications to help change the course of a country's thinking.

"I had this idea that people who worked in NGOs or politics were super-skilled, impossibly hardworking, perfect. Then I got to know people doing those jobs, and I discovered they're just normal," she said. "And when I saw that, I knew not to be afraid of trying to do something."

Up until 2019, the NGO had not received enough funding to provide Johanna with a full-time salary. For years, she hustled at various part-time jobs so she could continue dedicating time to Konsent.

When I asked her what has kept her going for a decade, despite all the challenges, she replied, "It's a good question, something I ask myself quite often. I just believe this needs to be done—that we still have a gap in the field of sexual violence prevention, and it hasn't been solved yet. If someone else were doing it, I wouldn't feel this urge to take it on myself. But no one else is, so I have to."

Johanna is often reminded why her work matters. People stop her on the street to thank her, telling her that what she does is important. Some people have told her they wish Konsent existed when they were younger, believing it could have helped them avoid violent and traumatic situations.

"Even boys have told me they are sorry they didn't know certain things earlier—that they wouldn't have behaved the way they did," she said. "And they are really sorry about it. This is the reason to carry on trying to make a world where sexual violence doesn't happen as often as it does."

CHAPTER 5

ALASTAIR LOGAN, ENGLAND

Around 6:00 p.m. on Saturday, October 5, 1974, a young lawyer named Alastair Logan locked up his office in Guildford, a quiet town around an hour south of London, and left for the day.

"When I got home, I saw on the news that two pubs had been bombed in Guildford," he said.

The first bomb went off at the Horse and Groom pub at 8:50 p.m., killing twenty-one-year-old civilian Paul Craig and four off-duty British soldiers: Ann Hamilton, age nineteen; Caroline Slater and William Forsyth, both eighteen; and John Hunter, seventeen. More than fifty people were injured. The second bomb detonated at the Seven Stars pub at 9:30 p.m., injuring eleven more people.

The attacks were the latest in a series of explosions and shootings by the Irish Republican Army (IRA) across Britain. In the previous twelve months, the IRA had planted bombs in and around London. The year before the Guildford bombs, the IRA decided to take its campaign to Britain, believing attacks there would get more attention than in Northern Ireland.

In the years before and after the attack, large-scale violence tore Northern Ireland apart. Peaceful protests began in the mid-1960s against discrimination in housing, employment, and voting rights, which generally disadvantaged the country's minority Catholic population. Most Catholics saw themselves as Irish nationalists despite being under British rule. Inspired partly by the US civil rights movement, some began marching for equality. The British government backed a violent crackdown ordered by Northern Ireland's political elite in response to the peaceful demonstrations and sent troops to "temporarily" restore order in 1969. Those soldiers remained for decades.

Meanwhile, the IRA saw itself as the defender of the Irish nationalist community in Northern Ireland and aimed to reunify Northern Ireland with southern Ireland, which had won independence from Britain fifty years earlier. The IRA launched what it called an armed struggle, while the British government defined it as terrorism.

No one knew in 1974 how long the violence would continue. But the Guildford attacks turned out to be in the early years of the conflict, which only ended with the Good Friday Agreement of 1998. Over three decades, thousands of people were killed, with many more injured and tens of thousands jailed.

While most of the violence was confined to Northern Ireland, it also spilled into the south of Ireland and across the Irish Sea into Britain. Five months before the Guildford attacks, on May 17, Loyalist paramilitaries—enemies of the IRA who wanted Northern Ireland to remain part of the United Kingdom—killed thirty-three people, including a pregnant woman, in the bombings of Dublin and Monaghan in the south of Ireland. Many others were injured. It was the deadliest day of the conflict.

The IRA started its London bombing campaign in 1973. Part of the IRA's frustration was that the conflict barely registered as a major issue with British voters. In two British general elections in 1974, the debates focused on the strength of labor unions and Britain's relationship with Europe. Despite regular news reports of British soldiers being killed or injured, the conflict occupied a strange, near-but-far place in British consciousness.

I first met Logan in 1989 when I was a young journalist, writing about the Guildford attacks and other related cases. In an article for the *Catholic Herald* that year, I described him as a "genial, bespectacled" man. When we met at his home in Sussex in the south of England in June 2025, Logan was just as warm as I remembered him from my first interview, and he still wore square-rimmed glasses clearly chosen for practicality over fashion.

Reflecting on the violence that erupted five decades ago, he admitted that the conflict had originally been something of a mystery to him.

"I knew nothing about Northern Ireland then," he said. "I wasn't even sure if it was a proper part of the United Kingdom. I'd heard about [prominent Protestant cleric and political leader] Ian Paisley, and I knew about the IRA, and that was it."

The IRA wanted to bring the war to the British mainland, targeting major cities and places where British soldiers socialized as well. "One bomb in London is worth one hundred in Belfast," a political pamphlet supporting the IRA said, highlighting the attention such attacks would draw. The IRA regarded soldiers' pubs as legitimate targets, even if civilians were also killed and injured, which is why Guildford's Horse and Groom and Seven Stars were bombed that Saturday night.

The following Monday, Alastair Logan was back at his desk, hard at work to make ends meet as the sole practitioner of his one-man law firm. He had qualified as a lawyer only six years earlier.

"I bought a law practice in 1971 from a very elderly solicitor. In those days, buying a practice was really the only way that you could shoehorn yourself into something that was working," he said. "I didn't realize that the man I bought it from was really not as competent as I'd thought, and the firm owed £11,000 in damages from various cases."

At the time, that £11,000 sum could have comfortably bought four semi-detached houses in Guildford.

"I had to raise that money out of my income," said Logan, "so I had a general practice principally doing legal aid work in crime and matrimonial as well as conveyancing. The local police would arrest someone for minor stuff like shoplifting, and I would get an offer from the court: 'Do you want to take this legal aid certificate?' And so that was a lot of my work."

Logan was from a highly respectable family. His grandfather had been appointed by Buckingham Palace as the Garter King of Arms, in charge of the nation's heraldry. One of these duties, upon the death of a monarch, was to proclaim the name of the new sovereign to the British Empire and the world. So in 1952, it was Logan's grandfather who officially announced that Princess Elizabeth would become Queen Elizabeth II.

Logan went to a private school in South London, founded by royal charter in 1829, and then to the prestigious University College London in the early 1960s. He says much of the radical student awakening of the era passed him by. His father, who had also been a lawyer, was by then principal of the University of London, responsible for the administration of a huge university with many constituent colleges, including the one Logan attended, which was another reason he stayed away from controversy. Logan was no fiery political activist. As a student, he lived with his parents and had short hair, when many of his peers were growing theirs long in rebellion.

By early December 1974, two months after the Guildford bombs, the local Surrey Police, helped by London's Metropolitan Police, were under enormous pressure to find the bombers. The Guildford attacks had been followed by more bombings, including one on November 7 at the King's Arms in Woolwich, another "soldiers' pub," closer to London. A soldier and a barman were killed, and thirty-five more people were injured. On November 21, more IRA bombs planted in pubs killed twenty-one people in Birmingham, Britain's second-largest city, just over one hundred miles north of London. Unlike in Guildford, where there had been no arrests, within twenty-four hours, the local West Midlands Police had taken into custody six men, who would be convicted of the bombings. Two months after the October 5 Guildford attacks, the Surrey Police still hadn't brought in any suspects. An anonymous tip changed everything.

The police soon arrested Paul Hill, a twenty-year-old man from Belfast, setting off an absurd, protracted, and tragic saga. The police tracked him down in Southampton, England, and took him into custody. New laws rushed through by Parliament in the aftermath of the Birmingham pub bombings allowed the police to hold and interrogate terrorism suspects for seven days—up from the previous two—before charging or releasing them, and to deny access to legal advice for up to seven days. Hill was the first person to be held under the new law. Under threats and violence at the hands of the police, Hill named all sorts of people he knew only vaguely, implicating them in the Guildford bombings, while confessing to the bombings himself and to the Woolwich attack.

Hill's fantasy confession named various friends and acquaintances, including twenty-four-year-old Paddy Armstrong and twenty-year-old Gerry Conlon. All three had gone to the same school in Catholic West Belfast. Like virtually all young men from Catholic neighborhoods, they had been frequently stopped for questioning by British soldiers. Armstrong's family home had been raided several times by British soldiers unsuccessfully looking for guns. Such aggressive searches were routine in the neighborhoods where the three had grown up. Four months before the Guildford bombings, Hill and Conlon had been picked up together in Belfast and questioned by British soldiers for a few hours before being released.

The three had met up in London occasionally, Conlon and Hill much more often than Armstrong. They were all living a vagabond life that bounced between short-term jobs, pubs, and betting shops. While Hill usually stayed with extended family, Armstrong lived in squats and experimented with drugs, as did Armstrong's English girlfriend, seventeen-year-old Carole Richardson.

By early December, they were all in police custody and quickly gained notoriety as the Guildford Four. Various other people were also rounded up, including Hill's pregnant girlfriend, Gina.

Soon after, Hill said his confessions were false. The police beatings and abuse he could have ridden out, he claimed, but when the police threatened to frame Gina for the murders at Guildford, he spun a wild story.

He initially refused to admit to any part in the Guildford bombings. He was then interviewed by two members of the Royal Ulster Constabulary, the police force in Northern Ireland. They threatened that if he did not confess, his mother would have an "accident." Hill admitted to the murder of Brian Shaw, a former British soldier, in Belfast six months before. Then the Surrey Police leaned on him hard. One of the officers pulled the trigger on an unloaded gun through the flap of Hill's cell door, and he was told his pregnant girlfriend would be charged with the Guildford bombings if he did not admit to being involved.

Hill confessed to taking part in the Woolwich and Guildford bombs. His ties to the IRA have never been publicly detailed, although he admitted in the 1980s he had been "involved" with the organization. It was also widely believed that after July 1974, the IRA wanted to question him on the whereabouts of a weapon, and he was trying to hide from them.

In his outlandish confession, Hill also named Conlon's forty-year-old aunt, Annie Maguire, as a senior bomb maker. The police consequently raided her London home, and despite finding no evidence of bomb making equipment, they arrested her; her husband, Patrick; their two children, thirteen-year-old Patrick and fifteen-year-old Vincent; her brother Sean Smyth; her brother-in-law Patrick "Giuseppe" Conlon (Gerry Conlon's father, who had come from Belfast after hearing of his son's arrest); and a family friend, Patrick O'Neill. They were all charged with explosives offenses and became known as the Maguire Seven. Armstrong, his girlfriend, Carole Richardson, and the Maguire Seven were all arrested on December 3. For the following week, said Armstrong, he was abused and beaten by the police, hung out of a second-floor window, and threatened that he would be killed if he did not admit to being involved.

Around 10:00 a.m., on Tuesday, December 10, Logan recalled, he was sitting alone in his office in Guildford when a legal aid clerk called him.

"She said, 'Do you want a legal aid certificate for one of the bombers?' That was exactly what she said. And I said no, because I was a sole practitioner and I thought it was going to be an enormous case. And I thought that the other firms in Guildford who had larger staff could manage it better. And then she rang me back after lunch about 2:00 p.m., and she said, 'Alastair, I've been around all the solicitors in Guildford, and none of them will touch it. Would you take it?' So I said, 'Yes, okay, I will.' I got Patrick Armstrong, capital A, top of the list."

The families of the other three of the Guildford Four had managed to find legal firms elsewhere. Logan was the only local lawyer from Guildford involved. He made an appointment to go and see

Patrick Armstrong the following morning. Logan had a decent working relationship with the local police at the station from handling petty crime cases. But this was very different.

"Detective Sergeant Donaldson met me in the entrance by the reception desk," Logan remembered. "He took me up through the sealed doors to the first floor, walked me down a corridor to a room where there were three police officers, including himself, and a man, Paddy Armstrong, sitting at a desk. He was shaking violently, and I thought, 'Oh, God.' And then I noticed that he had an injury to his eye. And I said to the officer, 'How did he get that?' And the officer said he fell down the steps in the cell complex. Well, I knew that the cell complex was all ground floor. There were no steps. And so I didn't believe him. And I shook hands with Armstrong. I told him who I was and why I was there and that I would be representing him in court."

Armstrong later recalled his feelings in that first meeting with Logan:

> After seven days, I barely know my own name. Nobody in my family knows where I am. Nobody in the world will know I'm missing except the people arrested with me. My face is cut, bruised, and unshaven. My clothes filthy. But now I'm in a room with a serious-looking man with a British accent and glasses. Alastair Logan shakes my hand. I'll find out later that he's more experienced in divorce proceedings than criminal cases. But I don't ask anything like that today. Right now, as far as I'm concerned, he's just another person who wants to make me look guilty.

Logan said Armstrong's strong Irish accent was almost impossible to understand: "I asked him if he wanted his relatives told about his arrest, and he said he did, and I asked him for the address of his mother, and I couldn't understand what he was talking about. I wrote down his mother's address in Belfast phonetically. He said that she didn't have a phone, and so I obviously would have to send a letter. The whole conversation was about seven, maybe ten, minutes."

Logan and Armstrong shook hands again as the lawyer left.

"I was walking back down the corridor with Donaldson," said Logan, "and Donaldson said to me, 'Do you want to use the facilities?' And I said, 'No, thanks.' He said, 'I think you will. You've shaken hands with him twice, and he's got scabies.' It was quite a way to prejudice someone against him. But as I was walking home, I was thinking to myself, 'If I can't understand this guy, how the hell do they understand him? They're English police officers.' I didn't even know yet that he'd made all these confessions; I hadn't seen any documents."

Already perturbed by Paddy Armstrong's injuries at the police station, Logan quickly spotted holes in the case when he reviewed the files. "When you looked at the statements the [Guildford] Four made, everybody was saying they were doing something that somebody else said they weren't doing. There were one hundred inconsistencies between the statements."

He soon realized the entire case relied on a dubious confession.

"And when you knew that the only evidence they had against Armstrong was his confession," Logan said, "that there were no forensics, there was no visual, that they didn't even put him on an identity parade, you got to the stage where you were saying to yourself, 'This is hooky,' and you began to get the impression that this confession was not a voluntary confession."

Armstrong's claim that policemen had hung him out of a second-floor window by his feet and told him they would drop him unless he confessed started to sound plausible. The other three also gave detailed accounts of how they had been threatened and violently abused by the police and forced to confess. But if the evidence was hooky, and the confession far from voluntary, it raised the horrifying prospect that the police had framed innocent people for murders.

In March 1975, six months after the bombings, the Four had a committal hearing in Guildford. During the lunch break, Logan and the legal representatives of the other three went to the local Wimpy Bar [a 1970s British burger chain].

"That was the first time I really said it out loud," said Logan, recalling what he said to the other lawyers. "I said, 'I have to tell you, I think my guy is innocent.' It was like saying something traitorous. And they all looked at me, and they said, 'Yeah, we think ours are, too.' It was a frightening thought, because the charges were horrendous, leading to massive life sentences if [our clients were] convicted. And you knew you were up against a 'he said, she said' situation with the police on one side and these four on the other."

The trial was set for September that year. As Logan tried to find out more about Armstrong's whereabouts on the night of the October 5 Guildford bombings, he visited some of the squats where Armstrong had stayed, hoping to find people who knew his client. The squatters didn't welcome strangers with posh accents asking questions.

At one house, Logan recalled, "I was calling out names and saying who I was, and somebody hit me from behind with a brick. I didn't lose consciousness, but there was a lot of blood."

By the time the trial came, Logan hoped at least Armstrong's girlfriend, Carole Richardson, would be acquitted. After all, she had an alibi for the night of the October 5 bombings. A guy called Frank Johnson said he was with her and her friend Lisa Astin at a gig in London, and there were photos to prove it.

"If Carole Richardson was found innocent, the rest of the cases could have collapsed like a house of cards," said Logan.

Johnson's evidence was a problem for the police because it completely exonerated Richardson. So the police arrested Johnson, beat him, and threatened to kill his disabled mother. They warned that they would charge him with the Guildford bombings unless he changed his story to say he met Richardson later that night. A later meeting would have theoretically given Richardson enough time to plant the bombs and return to London in time for the gig.

Under intense police pressure, Johnson made another statement giving a later time for the meeting with Richardson. When he appeared in court as a witness during the trial, Johnson bravely reverted to his original, truthful statement, insisting he had met Carole Richardson at the earlier time, but changing his story had damaged his credibility. The jury decided to believe the police. They found the Four—the three young Irishmen and the English teenager Carole Richardson—guilty of the Guildford bombing, while Hill and Armstrong were found guilty of the Woolwich bombing.

Armstrong was sentenced to thirty-five years in prison. The judge said if the Four had been convicted a decade earlier, they would have been sentenced to death. (The United Kingdom abolished the death penalty for murder in 1965.)

At that moment in court, Armstrong remembers feeling as though he were under water: "I don't yet understand the nuances or how unusual this is, but I get what [the judge] is saying. I will not be leaving prison for at least thirty-five years."

Conlon was sentenced to thirty years, Hill was sentenced to life, and Carole Richardson—because she had been a child at the time of the attacks—received an indefinite sentence.

Logan immediately started looking for grounds for an appeal, but prospects were bleak. The jury had believed the police, and their verdict was unanimous.

Logan privately told another lawyer, "I have no alternative but to pursue the matter on behalf of Armstrong, because if I do not, no one else will. . . . I owe a duty to Armstrong. I firmly believe that he had no connection whatsoever with the Guildford bombing. I sometimes think it would be easier for everyone if one did not have convictions and principles."

Then something extraordinary happened. Two months after the verdicts, exactly a year after Logan had first met Armstrong in the police station, the police chased four IRA men who had opened fire on a restaurant and trapped them in a flat in central London. They cornered the IRA men—Eddie Butler, Hugh Doherty, Harry Duggan, and Joe O'Connell—in Balcombe Street after they had broken into flat number 22B and taken a middle-aged couple hostage. The televised siege lasted a week before the men gave up the hostages and were arrested. Within forty-eight hours, some of those captured told police that they had carried out the bombings at Woolwich and Guildford the previous year, and they had no connection to those convicted.

The dramatic confessions posed quite a problem for the authorities. If these newly arrested men had done the bombings and the convicted were innocent, it raised awkward questions about why people in police custody had confessed to crimes they didn't commit. The police chose not to act on the new confessions.

Six months after he was arrested at Balcombe Street and had told the police about his part in the Guildford and Woolwich bombings, Joe O'Connell wrote to Logan from prison in London, asking for a meeting. Logan visited him and heard who the real bombers were. Logan then went to see another IRA man in prison, Brendan Dowd, who was regarded as the leader of the IRA unit until his arrest in July 1975.

Logan knew he had to be very careful in taking any statement from Dowd. He had to avoid being accused of suggesting things to the prisoner or asking leading questions.

"I made arrangements, I got a senior police officer who'd retired, I got a court stenographer, I interviewed Dowd and the others, and I got confessions from them that were so detailed they could only have come from the people who'd actually done the bombings," he said.

One of the details proving Dowd was the real bomber, and not Armstrong, was that Dowd clearly described two old men in the Horse and Groom pub that night carrying shopping bags. There had never been mention of the pair in any of the media reports, and only someone present in the pub at the time could have known they were there.

At their trial in January 1977, the IRA men caught at Balcombe Street refused to plead to the one hundred counts on the indictment because the charges did not include the Guildford and Woolwich bombings. Joe O'Connell made a statement from the dock:

> We are all four Irish Republicans. We have recognized this court to the extent that we have instructed our lawyers to draw the attention of the court to the fact that four totally innocent people—Carole Richardson, Gerry Conlon, Paul Hill, and Paddy Armstrong—are serving massive sentences for three bombings, two in Guildford and one in Woolwich, which three of us and another man now imprisoned [Brendan Dowd] have admitted that we did. The Director of Public Prosecutions was made aware of these admissions in December 1975 and has chosen to do nothing. We wonder if he will still do nothing when he is made aware of the new and important evidence which has come to light through the cross-examination by our counsel of certain prosecution witnesses in this trial.

O'Connell named scientists who he said played a vital part in the convictions of the innocent Guildford Four. He cited evidence that the police had deliberately ignored, showing he and his colleagues, not those convicted, had done the bombings. These new public confessions appeared to be the breakthrough that Logan was hoping for. But they were not. The four innocent people still remained in prison.

At the Guildford Four's appeal later that year, in October 1977, judges heard evidence from O'Connell and others. They decided that Dowd's team was guilty of the attacks, not *instead* of the Guildford Four, but *alongside* them. In other words, the judges invented a new theory unsubstantiated by evidence that at least eight people had carried out the bombings.

These were difficult times for the Four. And, of course, for Logan.

The failure of the appeal "came not as a surprise but as a great sadness," Logan said. "I was incredibly depressed and disappointed and felt I had been a party to something dishonest."

The case took a significant toll on Logan's personal life. In 1977, the far-right group the National Front sent a three-page letter to his home, threatening to kill him, describing in detail how they would do it.

"My wife opened the letter, and she rang the police," Logan said.

The letter had been carelessly passed around among various police officers and was covered in fingerprints, but it had been typed on a typewriter with some peculiarities and was posted from a very rural area of Wales.

"So an average police officer should have been able to figure out who wrote it, but they never followed it up," Logan continued. "They sort of thought it was a huge joke. It was really the straw that broke the camel's back for my wife. She made it a condition of the continuance of our marriage that I drop the case. I'm not entirely blaming her, but we divorced soon after."

There was no question of Logan's giving up on the case. He carried on throughout the next decade, unpaid, representing the Four, and in addition the Maguire Seven, who had been sentenced based on faulty forensic evidence to between four and fourteen years in prison.

"My father thought I was stupid for carrying on," said Logan. "He didn't try to stop me, but he thought I was stuffing up my career. Former clients crossed the street to avoid talking to me. I eventually became known as the IRA Lawyer."

It got so bad that British intelligence officers infiltrated Logan's office at night.

"I set traps," Logan recalled. "I would leave a pile of files on the desk, and I would adjust them in such a way that a ruler would touch each one of the files. And then I knew in the morning if somebody had moved them, and sometimes they had."

The appeals over the years were lost, and it was hard to generate new interest in the case. When journalists wanted to talk to Logan about other issues, he tried to make it on condition that they discussed the Guildford Four case first.

"I had some partial success," he said.

Many in authority knew they had the wrong people for the bombings but were still prepared to cover up the truth that the police had framed innocent people. And two years into Paddy Armstrong's sentence, prisoners broke into the administrative offices at Hull Prison during a riot. Armstrong got to see his files. Inside them, he read, "This man is believed to be innocent."

Logan struggled on, trying to get media attention for the wrongful convictions.

When I met with Logan in his Guildford office in early 1989, the Four were still in prison. Then, as now, his voice was a mix of determination and exasperation when talking about the cases.

"I knew right from the start, before the trial, they were innocent," he told me then.

When asked about working for free for all those years, he said, "I don't count it up; it's not all logged down in minutes spent working on the case in a ledger somewhere. It was just something someone had to do." Shrugging, he added that the "dark years" between 1977 and 1985 were "a struggle, because no one wanted to know."

But his doggedness helped persuade some influential people that the Four were innocent. After some years, Catholic Cardinal Basil Hume met Giuseppe Conlon in prison and became convinced that he was an innocent man. Hume then took up their case, along with a handful of retired senior politicians.

"Once the cardinal became involved, someone with impeccable credentials, it was obvious the case wasn't just being publicized for political reasons. Still, I shouldn't have had to spend years guarding the fluttering flame in the hope that I could influence important people," said Logan.

Thanks in part to pressure from the cardinal and others, a new appeal was set for the Four in October 1989—fourteen years after their convictions.

"New evidence emerged that Conlon had an alibi, as he had said at the original trial. The police had interviewed his alibi witnesses in early 1975 and concealed these statements with the assistance of Crown Counsel. We also had new alibi evidence for Paul Hill and Carole Richardson," said Logan.

In mid-October 1989 Logan took another unexpected phone call.

"Someone from the court told me the prosecution had an urgent appointment before the Lord Chief Justice the day after tomorrow. And I said, 'What is it?, He said, 'I can't tell you. I've been told I can't tell you. But it's good news.' So I knew that the prosecution was tossing in their hand, and at that, the Four were going to get out."

Later that day, Armstrong, Conlon, and Hill were all brought together, without explanation, to the same prison in London.

"I heard two blokes saying the Guildford Four were getting out on Thursday," recalled Armstrong.

Then the radio in the prison broadcast the news that they were to be released.

A couple of days later, on October 19, 1989, the Four were brought to court.

"And then we went up to the dock," said Armstrong. "And the first person I seen was my younger sister, and I hadn't seen her for fourteen years."

The cover-up was finally falling apart.

"What had been discovered in the Surrey Police files were documents that proved the police had lied in their statements and under oath," said Logan. "The detention sheets produced at the trial were shown to be forgeries involving no less than thirty-two Surrey Police officers. Notes were found of two interviews of Hill, which he had testified had taken place, and which were denied under oath by the officers concerned. And drafts of the 'contemporaneous' record of Armstrong's confession were found, proving the document to be a forgery. As the Lord Chief Justice said on quashing the convictions, 'The police must have lied.'"

Faced with the prospect of having their lies and perjury revealed in court, the prosecution simply said they didn't want to contest the appeal. The Four were free.

I was with hundreds of others outside the Old Bailey court in London that day. Supporters, curious tourists, passers-by, and construction workers on a break waited to see what would happen. Gerry Conlon suddenly stormed out of the building, punching the air. He had been released. Flanked by his sisters, he gave a passionate speech about how he had watched his innocent father die in prison, and how the Maguires and others were wrongly imprisoned. He spoke of fifteen years stolen from his life. The police outside the court, confronted by an increasingly angry crowd of the Four's supporters, gave up trying to control us. Armstrong slipped out the back, away from the crowds.

While the hearing was a triumph for Logan and the other defense lawyers, they also felt cheated out of a full appeal in which the police lies would have been laid bare for the public to see. Some of those who had criticized Logan for sticking with the case for fifteen years now congratulated him, including his father.

"The president of the Law Society actually wrote to me, which was surprising," said Logan. "And a couple of people I knew who had become judges. Some people locally said, 'well done,' that sort of thing, people who previously might not have been too enthusiastic about what I was doing."

The victory came too late for Logan's clients in many respects, however.

"My clients Armstrong and Richardson were both seriously damaged by their convictions and time in prison," said Logan. "They desperately needed to have professional psychiatric help to enable them to live after their release. Two psychiatrists who had examined them in prison advocated that they should go quietly into oblivion to avoid the press and to receive the treatment they needed. And that was what happened. It enabled them to reintegrate successfully. Both married and had children. Both suffered from PTSD for the rest of their lives, but the outcome might have been very different."

On release from prison that day, Armstrong had nowhere to go, so Logan took him in.

"What else could I do?" said the lawyer. At home, Logan said, "I could keep an eye on him, and he needed to adjust, and he also needed to have psychological support."

Armstrong stayed with Logan for six months, learning how to live outside prison. Logan taught him how to cross the road, how to shop, and how to handle money.

The arrests of six men in the immediate aftermath of the 1974 Birmingham pub bombings, which heaped pressure on the police in Guildford to find suspects, turned out to be as problematic as the cases of the Guildford Four and the Maguire Seven. Known as the Birmingham Six, the men were each sentenced to life in prison for the murders of twenty-one people. But they were innocent, and like the Guildford Four, had been framed. Following a campaign for their release, and new evidence showing they had been convicted based on faulty forensic evidence and forced confessions, they were all exonerated and freed from prison, their convictions quashed in 1991.

Carole Richardson spent much of her time in jail at the maximum-security wing for women at Durham Prison in the north of England with Judy Ward, also arrested in 1974 and wrongly convicted of an IRA bomb attack, in which twelve British soldiers and their families were killed in a bus explosion. Ward was sentenced to twelve life terms and thirty years of imprisonment. She had also been convicted because of her false confessions and was finally exonerated and freed in 1992.

In 2013, a very ill Frank Johnson asked to see Logan. Johnson had provided an alibi for Carole Richardson for the night of the Guildford bombing, but was forced to change his story under police coercion. He never forgave himself. Johnson died a week after they met, at age sixty-three.

"He had PTSD, he was feeling incredibly guilty," said Logan. "He would burst into tears, and he felt that he was responsible for those imprisoned."

Giuseppe Conlon, Gerry Conlon's father, who had been arrested with the Maguire household, died in prison of tuberculosis in 1980 after a long illness. His release on parole was granted by the British government the day he died. When no British airline would agree to fly his coffin back to Ireland, Logan arranged for the Irish airline Aer Lingus to take his body home.

An Oscar-nominated 1993 movie, *In the Name of the Father,* starring Daniel Day-Lewis, gave a version of the ordeal of the Guildford Four and the Maguire Seven, focusing on the relationship between Giuseppe and Gerry Conlon.

Paddy Armstrong, age seventy-two, lives in Ireland, and in 2022 was diagnosed with dementia.

Gerry Conlon died from cancer at age sixty in 2014.

Carole Richardson died from cancer at age 55 in 2012.

Paul Hill lives in the United States.

Patrick Maguire was thirteen when he was wrongfully arrested in 1974 and was sentenced to four years in an adult prison. The Maguire Seven had their convictions quashed in 1991.

The Maguire Seven and the Guildford Four received a public apology from Prime Minister Tony Blair in 2005.

It never occurred to Logan to give up the case, even after his clients were exonerated. He wanted the decades of corruption that had led to their wrongful convictions to be exposed and for those responsible to be held accountable.

"I knew that the police had achieved the convictions through crime, and the officers had not been held to account for it. They intimidated them, they frightened the shit out of them to get them to confess. They got confessions, which were mutually inconsistent. There was no other evidence against them, so they then started a cover-your-ass project."

Confronted with public outrage that the police had framed eleven innocent people, immediately after the Four were freed, the British government commissioned an inquiry into what had happened. Senior Judge Sir John May was appointed to head an investigation into the police's conduct.

"In the inquiry, the Maguire case was heard in public, but the Guildford case was heard in secret, and none of the Four were permitted to attend any of the hearings or be represented at the hearings," said Logan.

To make matters even worse, in December 2019, a few days before seven hundred files from the inquiry were supposed to be made public, the authorities decided they should stay closed until 2059. These include original interview notes and records of the Four's detention.

Fifty years on from the wrongful convictions, Logan is battling to have the papers from the Sir John May Inquiry and another document, the Habershon Report, released to help show what really happened. Nine days into the Guildford Four's five-week trial in 1975, Senior Metropolitan Police Officer Commander Roy Habershon, an expert on bombings, sent a report to the prosecution. In it, he detailed how the same IRA unit responsible for the Guildford and Woolwich bombs had carried out dozens of other attacks. He showed multiple links connecting all the bombings, including fingerprints. The report identified an entirely different team of people as responsible for the crimes, effectively exonerating the Four. But it was never shown to the jury or to their lawyers. The full Habershon Report has also been kept from the public.

Three police officers from Guildford eventually faced trial in 1993, charged with conspiracy to pervert the course of justice. They included John Donaldson, who had met Logan that day in December 1974 and suggested he wash his hands after meeting Armstrong.

The police officers were all acquitted, their defense lawyers suggesting Armstrong had, in fact, been guilty all along. Logan described their trial as "a nonsense of a criminal trial, a con trick." He said the police "lied on an industrial scale. It took thirty-two officers to forge the detention sheets. So thirty-two of Surrey's finest were committing forgery."

In 2022, an inquest into the Guildford bombings refused to look beyond the immediate cause of death of the victims. While the Surrey Police were given free legal representation, none of the survivors or bereaved families were granted legal aid.

No one has been prosecuted for the Guildford or Woolwich bombings since the Four were released in 1989.

Logan's career has not focused exclusively on this case. He was also a lawyer for Harry Roberts, convicted of killing two police officers in 1966. Logan obtained his release after Roberts had served forty-eight years in jail. He also helped train the police in new interrogation techniques that didn't rely on force. But it is his persistence for more than five decades on the cases of the Guildford Four and the Maguire Seven that he is best known for.

The most important outcome now, he says, is the release of the Habershon Report and the papers from the Sir John May Inquiry.

"People talk about miscarriages of justice, as if they're an accident," he said. "That's not what happened in the Guildford case. It didn't go wrong. It went right. The police got the conviction because they set out on a criminal enterprise, and they were successful."

Looking back, Logan says he blames himself in the early days for seeing the Guildford and Woolwich bombings in isolation and not linking them to the other IRA attacks at the time.

"Other bombings were taking place," he noted. "Clearly, my guy wasn't involved because he was locked up, but I wasn't curious enough to inquire about what these explosions and shootings were, because then it might have become clear that there was a commonality in evidence which linked the Guildford case to whoever was still doing the bombings. But of course, we didn't get the arrest of the Balcombe Street people until December 1975."

When I asked Logan if what happened in 1974 seems like a lifetime ago, he replied, "Not quite, because it's still very vivid. It's still going. My problem, of course, is that the hourglass is running down, and I don't think there'll be anybody to take it on if I stop."

CHAPTER 6

IRYNA FEDORIV, UKRAINE

One evening in 2009, Iryna Fedoriv heard a knock at her apartment door. It was her neighbors Yulia and Viktoria. She asked them in and offered them tea. Impromptu visits like this were a normal part of life in Kotsiubynske, a tight-knit suburb of Kyiv, where everyone seemed to know everything about one another. Iryna, twenty-five years old at the time, was working at a national television station called STB as chief of the information analysis department, producing TV news. She had moved into the modest seventh-floor apartment two years earlier.

The two women knew that she worked in television. Iryna hadn't told them, but in her small village, which covers one and one-half square miles and has a population of about twenty thousand, news traveled fast. That night, they told her that the village council had begun awarding freshly created one-hundred-hectare homesites in the local Bilychanskyi Forest to friends and relatives. In 2009, the forest had no legal or environmental protections, but it had never been the property of the village, so the whole idea of carving up and transferring plots to private owners was widely seen as unlawful. The women told Iryna that a group of about ten locals was trying to stop it.

Iryna's neighbors had come around that evening not for chitchat but with a specific request: They asked her to arrange a TV exposé on the forest's being subdivided and sold off. Iryna agreed, thinking that if her station's coverage aired, the developers would be exposed.

In 2012, activists picketed the office of then-Ukrainian President Viktor Yanukovych, demanding that the forest be granted the highest level of environmental protection. At the time, Yanukovych stated that the six-thousand-hectare forest of pine and oak must be preserved as the "lungs" of the Kyiv region. It has long been enjoyed by locals and visitors as a virtual oasis offering relief from the gray Soviet-style brutalism of the city's commuter belt.

For generations, lovers, parents and toddlers, and the elderly have strolled along the narrow pathways, past lakes and ponds and beaver dams, shaded by overhanging branches and leafy greenery on either side. Dog walkers let their pets race around freely. Hundreds of plant and animal species have thrived there for millennia. The forest also has a treasured historical significance: During the Second World War, it served as a buffer zone to defend the capital by hindering enemy movement and by giving shelter to local residents and partisan fighters resisting Nazi occupation.

I first met Iryna in the summer of 2021, when she gave me a guided tour of the forest. She even made me pose for pictures next to the famous floating tree, its trunk seemingly suspended in midair. The long struggle to have the forest protected from developers was nearing an end, but the journey had been difficult, with many dangerous setbacks for her and others involved in the campaign.

When we met again four years later in war-torn Kyiv, Iryna remembered how it had all begun with the 2009 knock on the door, and how being young and working at the famous STB television station had given her a heady sense of power.

"We were goddamn television gods," she shouted, throwing her hands out in front of her and laughing. "I thought, 'Yeah, no problem, we'll do a report about this forest and millions of people will see it, and the problem will be solved.' This was before the advent of social media. There weren't many cable TV channels. I mean, we'd sit around every morning deciding what the whole country would watch on TV that evening."

Things didn't go as Iryna anticipated. Her channel produced several reports on the local land grab. Then they produced a dozen more, but that didn't stop the developers.

When the media coverage failed to solve the problem, and the village council continued to sell off plots of the forest, locals urged Iryna to stand as a candidate for the 2010 council elections.

"But it was dangerous," noted Iryna. "We all knew that people who stood up to the oligarchs could have their cars set on fire. It was possible to self-nominate, to stand as an independent, not for a party, but I had to check with my workplace first because it might have been awkward for a journalist to go into politics."

Ukraine's oligarchs have historically wielded enormous influence, using their business clout to fund parties and shape laws and their media empires to suppress dissent. For decades, Ukrainians have seen oligarchic power and corruption as a major threat to the country. In 2008, Ukraine ranked 134th out of 180 countries on Transparency International's Corruption Perceptions Index, reflecting the widespread corruption in public institutions. Activists, journalists, and officials who oppose the oligarchs have faced threats, harassment, and even death.

Iryna's office gave her the go-ahead to run for one of the twenty-six seats on the village council.

"This was small-scale, very low-level, an unpaid job. I mean, the election district I was running for was basically just my apartment block and the one next door," Iryna said.

Two of her colleagues also ran for the council, to help save the forest, to show solidarity, and to help protect Iryna by making sure she wouldn't be the only target of pressure from the oligarchs.

"We knew there was no chance we were going to win," Iryna said. "It was about trying to get this issue of the forest talked about and showing how a campaign might work."

They wrote letters by hand and delivered them to everyone in the district.

"It was important for people to see it was really us writing the letters, not some orchestrated campaign," explained Iryna. "We didn't have any money to spend on campaigning, and this way, we didn't need any."

Against overwhelming odds, Iryna won.

"My god, I was shocked. It only took me about fifty votes to win, but I was so shocked. So there I was, suddenly a village deputy for a five-year term, a politician." She laughed. "I was the only one of the twenty-six elected who had campaigned to save the forest. Everyone else was against me."

Iryna's goal was to secure legal protection for the forest by having it declared a national park, which would prohibit its sale for private development. But that decision could only be made by the national government—a power far beyond that of a local village deputy.

"So I decided to go straight to the top," Iryna said, laughing again at her early naivete.

Iryna collected around fifteen thousand signatures on a petition to protect the forest. In 2012, a visiting French television crew wanted an interview with President Yanukovych for a movie they were making. Iryna helped organize the filming of the movie in Ukraine, including securing access to the president. And she shrewdly agreed to join the French crew for the interview as an interpreter.

"I went with the French journalists to the president's offices, and at the end of the interview, with the cameras still rolling, I jumped up and gave him the petition," she said. "I asked him to promise that the forest would be protected. He was taken a bit by surprise, but he said yes, and so we had him on film, saying the forest was safe."

Yanukovych wasn't generally known for his progressive politics. Although Iryna had cheekily managed to get his agreement to protect the forest, he was widely seen as a friend of the oligarchs. He represented the pro-Russian Party of Regions, and had presided over a crackdown on journalists, an effort to undermine the judiciary, and the jailing of political opponents.

The next day, she tried the same move on Prosecutor General Viktor Pshonka, visiting his office and telling him the president had promised to protect the forest.

"I asked if he would confirm that, and of course I had put him in an awkward position, so he said, 'Yes, if the president says so. . .'"

Iryna was delighted.

"It was like magic. We got promises on the record from the president and the prosecutor general. Plots of land in the forest had already been surveyed and fenced off for building, but no construction had begun, so we thought we'd saved the forest," she explained.

The developers were not going to give up without a fight, however. They promptly took the issue to court.

That same year, Iryna began to receive threatening phone calls.

"Some man phoned me one night, just before midnight, warning me that bad things could happen to me or my family. I reported the call at once to my office," recalled Iryna. "They said my family and I should move out of my apartment and away from the area. But I refused. For a few weeks, the TV station provided armed guards who lived with us."

Next, Iryna went to the police.

"A senior government official, a deputy minister, even came to my house to show me mug shots of people I should report to the authorities immediately," Iryna said. "Then he showed me some phone tracking data about the threats made to me, showing the physical location of the person who called me, and who they called next. I believe it was a developer and a mid-level politician."

But having stood strong against the threats and won a commitment from the president to save the forest, Iryna believed all that was needed was for the president to sign the papers, declaring the forest part of the Holosiivskyi National Nature Park. Iryna said she heard from sources in the president's office that the documents were ready for signing, but a tussle was going on among his staff between those who wanted him to sign and those who did not.

Then came Ukraine's Euromaidan Revolution (also known as the Revolution of Dignity). In late November 2013, under pressure from Russia, President Yanukovych announced he would not sign an Association Agreement with the European Union, a landmark deal that would have strengthened Ukraine's ties with Europe. Instead, he signaled closer alignment with Russia. Public unrest erupted into mass protests, which became known as the Euromaidan movement.

The dissent soon became the largest democratic movement in Europe since 1989. Protestors demanded greater democratic reforms and an end to widespread government corruption. Despite the bitterly cold winter, the street demonstrations carried on for months, and by the new year of 2014, they had grown even bigger.

Like many young people in Ukraine, Iryna joined the demonstrations. She said locals were bringing firewood from the forest to the protestors to burn during the painfully cold nights, when temperatures fell to minus 10 degrees Fahrenheit. They transported the wood in expensive Lexus cars to avoid being stopped at security checkpoints, as no one suspected rich people of supporting the revolution. The protests convulsed the country as pro-democracy demonstrators pushed for Ukraine to turn westward. In response,

Yanukovych's security forces lashed out violently, killing almost one hundred demonstrators in February 2014. The violence exposed the president's rapidly weakening control of the country, and he soon escaped to Russia.

While his departure was generally seen as a victory for those protesting corruption, Yanukovych fled before signing the crucial documents designating the forest as a national park. Later that year, acting President Oleksandr Turchynov did sign the documents, but little changed, said Iryna, because the decree still needed funding to take effect, and no money was allocated.

Iryna and her supporters were back to square one. As she restarted her campaign, the intimidation against her resumed as well. Her car tires were slashed, and she received regular abuse on social media. Even as a lone voice, she pushed to make the business of the local council more transparent, so that shady deals couldn't be made in secret.

"I started posting what we were discussing in the meetings on Facebook, and who voted for what," she remembered. "The council deputies used to hold the meetings in a small room, and none of the local people went to see what was happening. I started writing on a website about what was going on in the council meetings, and I was really surprised that people started to pay attention and then come to the meetings. It was marvelous. There weren't enough chairs for everyone showing up."

Meanwhile, at the national level, the revolution had sparked a wave of optimism and a push for change. Ukraine soon held fresh elections and launched new anti-corruption measures, creating new institutions such as the National Anti-Corruption Bureau (NABU) and the Specialized Anti-Corruption Prosecutor's Office (SAPO), designed to investigate and prosecute high-level corruption without political interference. Iryna decided not to run again, but she supported neighbors who were part of the campaign to save the forest to stand for office.

The 2015 elections were a success, with the forest campaigners winning some seats on the council. A new mayor was elected who wanted to make the sessions public. Now that the campaigners had some local power, Iryna urged them to make the village council meetings more transparent by holding them in the largest public hall in the village.

"We made the councilors turn around and face the people instead of sitting with their backs to them," said Iryna. "We filmed and streamed all the meetings. We made it as unpleasant as possible for those who had a vested interest in destroying the forest."

Even so, the councilors who opposed Iryna and her supporters tried unsuccessfully to force votes to replace the mayor.

What followed were public hearings on whether the community wanted the village to be officially incorporated into the city of Kyiv, a move that would provide the forest with greater protection. The village council would have no authority to parcel out the land or fence it off for proposed hotels, office complexes, or any other development.

"It was a very intense time. We didn't trust the other side to accept the official result. Even when we won with 61 percent of the vote, we were fearful that the official paperwork recording the votes might be stolen or tampered with. We had to protect all of it." Iryna laughed. "We had to get the documents out of the building safely, so several of us women went to the toilet, stuffed the papers down our bras, and walked out," she explained to me, miming pushing the documents down inside the top of her dress.

They had outmaneuvered the developers again. Those trying to protect the forest were winning, but the fight went on for years, as did the backlash. Some of Iryna's neighbors who supported the campaign had their cars set on fire.

Iryna said the attacks on her intensified after the 2015 elections. In 2016, someone with a knife tried to break into a room in her apartment block where Iryna used to edit a community newsletter. In June 2017, two men slashed the tires of her car. Distressingly, she said, the attack didn't happen in the middle of the night; according to CCTV footage, it happened at 8:50 a.m., when parents are taking their children to kindergarten.

"My family could easily have encountered these armed men," Iryna said.

That same month, Liudmyla Demchenko, a retired woman who was an important local election official and one of the forest's most vocal local supporters, was severely beaten near her home. Next, someone removed the security cameras outside Iryna's home. Then, in May 2018, the electricity to her apartment was cut, and her electricity meter was stolen from near the entrance to her block.

In July 2020, Iryna received a truly bizarre death threat. I have reported for many years on death threats against activists on every continent. Sometimes threats are made on social media, sometimes by a phone call. In other instances, it's an old-fashioned note slipped under the door or a message passed on through "a friend." But I have never seen a threat like the one made against Iryna.

"I was out one evening at a protest at the parliament about the push to make our village part of Kyiv, and afterward I went home to drink tea," she said. "And as I was about to walk in the door of my apartment building, I saw a freshly installed plaque on the wall by the entrance. Like a gray memorial plaque, in someone's honor. It had my picture on it. And it said Iryna Fedoriv used to live there."

Iryna took some pictures of the plaque and went upstairs to her apartment. When she went back downstairs to meet the police, she saw that her neighbors had already pulled the plaque loose and smashed it.

"I was like, 'No, that could have had fingerprints or evidence on it, you should have left it there,'" said Iryna. "I still have the bits in my basement."

Those trying to kill the campaign to protect the forest were clearly becoming desperate as more and more people joined the movement and resistance grew stronger. In 2021, the decree to designate the forest a national park was finally implemented. Still, the developers didn't give up, taking the case to the Supreme Court in the middle of Russia's war on Ukraine.

During those years, Iryna worked at CHESNO, an anti-corruption organization in Ukraine, using her media skills as the chief editor of their website to push for greater political transparency. Then in 2023, she co-founded Holka (The Needle), an NGO also focused on fighting corruption.

"The Needle has a very diverse purpose. It can pierce, unstitch, and expose what people want to hide, like corrupt schemes, but it can also stitch together people from different sectors into a single community. It's small but powerful," she said. "It can also cause a bit of pain if it has to."

The NGO tracks the activities of members of parliament, including their finances, voting records, and conflicts of interest. Restrictions imposed under martial law, introduced after Russia's full-scale invasion, and the increased centralization of power have made Iryna's work more important than ever.

"The parliament is closed to the public, to people like us," she said. "We can't walk in like before. It's like my days on the village council when things were done in secret and deals were made behind closed doors."

In March 2024, after a hard-fought struggle, Ukraine's Supreme Court finally ruled in favor of those protecting the forest, declaring that Kotsiubynske is, "in fact, an enclave within the territory of the city of Kyiv. . . ." This ruling meant unequivocally that the village council had no right to parcel out the land or fence it off for proposed hotels, office complexes, or any other development. The ruling was a momentous victory for the locals who had campaigned for sixteen years.

Iryna said the forest had provided an important part of the natural defense of Kyiv when Russian troops tried to attack the city from the west in early 2022. Although Russian soldiers temporarily took the suburban towns of Bucha and Irpin, they didn't manage to get past the forest and into the city of Kyiv. Preserving the forest, with its dense undergrowth, bogs, and swamps, undoubtedly helped repel the invasion.

Iryna admitted there were times when she had doubted herself.

"When I was on the village council and all these people around me, grown-up, adult people, were just disagreeing with me, I began to wonder. You start to ask yourself, maybe something is wrong with you and not with them," she said. "Those were five hard years. I was trying to be a good council member, but you start to examine yourself. With all those people always against you, sometimes you think deep down maybe you're the crazy one."

There was also pressure from family and friends, who worried about what was best for her.

"Some of them would ask, 'Do you really need all this stress? The attacks on you? You can go and work in the media somewhere, you don't need to do this activism, just forget about having that sort of energy.' Sometimes it makes you think," she said.

Nevertheless, like so many other activists, Iryna was prepared from an early age to be the odd one out. She was brought up in Chernihiv, a Russian-speaking city in the northeast of Ukraine, about forty miles from the Russian border. As in much of eastern Ukraine, Russian was the dominant language.

"Everyone at school spoke Russian, but at home, we spoke Ukrainian. It was like living a double life. Our family sort of lived like vampires," said with a laugh. "Being one thing at home and talking in Ukrainian, and another as soon as we stepped outside."

It was a genuine awakening when Iryna realized not everyone had to switch languages.

"My dad died when I was sixteen. We went to the west of Ukraine to bury him where he was born and where most of his relatives still lived. I saw people speaking Ukrainian openly in the streets, in shops, just in everyday life, not hiding it. It was a shock," she recalled.

The trip changed Iryna, and when she returned to school, she started to speak Ukrainian.

"Some of the teachers collected money to buy extra books in English for us from the Petrivka market in Kyiv. It was great for us," Iryna said. "But then I asked, 'How come we have English books in our library but no books in Ukrainian?'"

Iryina said the library was also missing books on Ukrainian history, including about the Holodomor, Stalin's man-made famine in the 1930s that killed millions of Ukrainians living under Soviet rule. She decided to take action.

"I started a sort of book club, but really, it was an excuse to buy books," Iryna recalled. "We got donations from the students, like twenty *kopiikas* [a few cents] at a time. When the teachers went back to the market, we'd collected enough money for them to buy two Ukrainian books. The next time, three books."

The literary collection had started.

"We had a special shelf in the school library," said Iryna, holding out her hands a couple of feet apart. There were so few books that the club members could only take one Ukrainian book home for one night.

Iryna saw the book campaign as an early lesson in activism that set her on the path to fighting for the forest.

"People's brains like fixing these sorts of problems," she said. "I thought we could fix the forest problem with two TV shows. That was a mistake, so you try again. You run in the village election, just to educate people in the process, not to win, and that was another mistake, because I won. So you move on, learning and making mistakes."

The war has also strengthened support for the fight against corruption, which remains a major obstacle to Ukraine's aspirations to join the EU and NATO.

"We are all fighting together. We are defending ourselves from Russia, and we are working to improve our country from the inside. Many experts are collaborating with us," Iryna said.

Despite the growing solidarity, Iryna's work has continued to make powerful enemies. Like many activists in Ukraine and elsewhere, Iryna has been hit with Strategic Lawsuits Against Public Participation (SLAPPs)—civil cases about alleged defamation that can lead to demands for huge compensation. Iryna has also had a criminal case brought against her and faces an ongoing online smear campaign.

"It's part of the job," she said, shrugging. "These things are designed partly to intimidate others from doing what I do."

Almost two decades after Yulia and Viktoria knocked on her door, Iryna is recognized as one of Ukraine's most effective civic activists.

"You just have to keep at it," she said, twisting an imaginary Rubik's Cube between her fingers, "and find ways to solve the problem, adjusting things until it works."

CHAPTER 7

LORENA FORNASIR AND GIAN ANDREA FRANCHI, ITALY

It's around seven thirty on an evening in late summer of 2025, and I'm in a small square in the Italian city of Trieste. As usual, Lorena Fornasir is also here. There are hundreds of people, mostly migrant men, sitting around on the small concrete ledges around the grass, some staring at their phones. About a dozen teenage scouts, boys and girls in blue uniforms with badges showing their associations, chat with the migrant men.

It's a calm, quiet scene. Two benches next to each other in the center of the piazza are covered in golden thermal blankets. Lorena sits on the edge of a bench and leans over to tend to the feet of a man in his twenties who sits next to her. He's wearing blue tracksuit bottoms and a black T-shirt with a numeral "1" on the back below the name Dinesh.

Lorena is wearing a white blouse, a black-and-white skirt, and matching white sandals. Her wrist jangles with a stack of bracelets, and a pearl necklace rests against her blouse. Her hands are covered with black medical gloves as she props her glasses on her nose and peers at the man's foot, assessing the damage. She reaches into a small green shopping cart covered with a Palestinian flag. It's full of bandages, gauze, wipes, Band-Aids, and other medical supplies, and as Lorena chats to the man, she expertly treats his feet, wiping between his toes before bandaging his left foot. Next to her on another bench, a friend of hers, a woman about the same age, cleans and rebandages the feet of another man. Walking for days in flip-flops has left his feet wounded and raw.

When Lorena has finished, another man steps forward, this time with an injured finger. After him, Lorena tends to a man whose feet aren't cut, but she cleans them anyway, then massages and gently straightens his cramping toes. She has treated thousands of people like this.

Lorena's work here began more than ten years ago. One day in 2015, the retired psychotherapist and her husband, Gian Andrea Franchi, a former philosophy teacher, were driving in Pordenone, a small city in northern Italy where they were living.

"Suddenly, we came across a line of people in the street with injured feet and wounds everywhere on their bodies," recalled Lorena. "I just got out of the car and started talking to them, asking them who they were, and hugging them, reassuring them, and giving them whatever I happened to have with me. When you see someone in danger or in need, do you have to think about it twice? No, we just acted immediately."

Gian Andrea and Lorena, who were eighty and sixty at the time, respectively, have been working to help migrants ever since.

"How can you just go back to the comfort of your own home when you have seen what we've seen?" Lorena asked.

Over the past decade, the pair have helped thousands of migrants who have made perilous journeys from war-ravaged countries and other dangerous places to Trieste, a port city with a rich intellectual, literary, and academic history in the far northeast of Italy, which is now their home. The Irish writer James Joyce lived there for twelve years more than a century ago. In a letter in 1909, Joyce described his return to the city as finding his "soul's peace."

In recent years, Trieste has become a key entry point for hundreds of thousands of migrants taking the Balkan route from the Middle East, South Asia, and Africa via Bulgaria, Turkey, Greece, and other countries (especially those that were part of the former Yugoslavia) to reach the European Union. Though migration peaked in 2015 during the Syrian civil war, the route still sees significant numbers of people trying desperately to reach safety. Trieste is only five miles from the border with Slovenia, and by the time many migrants arrive, they have been traveling on foot through five or more countries for months or even years.

Across the road from the city's small railway station, at the Piazza della Libertà (Liberty Square), Lorena and Gian Andrea have welcomed the migrants with water, food, and medicine almost every evening since 2015. The piazza is a modest public square by Italian standards. In the center stands a large statue of former Austrian Empress Elisabeth, a nod to Trieste's complicated heritage as part of the Austrian Empire. Office workers come to eat their lunch on one of a dozen benches in the shade of the trees. There is a water fountain nearby, and sea birds swoop down on the recycling bins near the bronze empress, scavenging scraps.

An important part of the work Lorena and Gian Andrea do is treating migrants' feet, which have been wounded from walking for countless miles in poorly made shoes that are soon falling apart. By the time many migrants reach Trieste, they are walking barefoot. Sometimes, Lorena and Gian Andrea see a handful of arrivals. Other times, there are hundreds. The couple stays in the square until everyone has been tended to, often until the early hours of the morning. The temperature reaches 40 degrees Celsius (104 degrees Fahrenheit) on some days and can plunge to minus 10 degrees Celsius (14 degrees Fahrenheit) at night.

The piazza is fifty steps from the railway station, where there are discreet reminders of the city's dark past. One commemorative plaque reads "Deported men, women, and children began from here the journey to the Nazi camps, September 1943–February 1945." Another nearby plaque reads "From this station in the twenty months of German occupation (1943–1945), most of the transports of death left direct from Italy to the Nazi death camps."

During the Second World War, Trieste had the only concentration camp in Italy with a crematorium, housed in a former rice-husking facility called the Risiera di San Sabba. Thousands of partisans, Jews, and political opponents of the Nazi regime were killed there. The facility was also used as a transit point for those being sent to their deaths at Auschwitz and elsewhere. At the end of the war, the city was divided—overseen by the victorious British and American forces from the west and by the Soviet-aligned Yugoslavian partisans from the east.

Over the last decade, the EU has cracked down on migrants seeking to enter its borders safely. Reaching Europe has become increasingly difficult for those fleeing wars. The option of crossing the Mediterranean Sea by boat is even more dangerous; in 2024, 2,573 people died attempting the journey, according to the International Organization for Migration. Many more people are walking hundreds of miles up through the Balkan countries and into Italy. More than one million people have taken this route since 2015.

The Balkan route is no easy option, however. With EU border policies growing increasingly restrictive and choking off ways people can apply for political asylum, migrants are being pushed into covert and hazardous routes, many of which are controlled by criminal gangs. The journey to Italy involves crossing mountains, dense forests, and rivers. At least four hundred migrants have died on this journey since 2014, mostly from road accidents, drowning, and violence. Many bodies will never be found. In August 2024, twelve migrants, including a baby, drowned after their boat capsized on the Drina River at the border of Bosnia and Herzegovina and Serbia. Others have been killed while walking across minefields in Bosnia.

The increasingly violent behavior of border guards along the route—including illegal "pushbacks" from one country back to another—and attacks by police dogs are forcing people to avoid the authorities, driving them into the hands of dangerous people smugglers. Once under the control of the smugglers, they are at risk of being kidnapped and held for ransom. Some people are sold into sexual slavery. Despite the dangers and the risk of severe trauma, many people are still managing to make their way to Trieste. While some intend to stay in Italy, most will go deeper into the EU—to Germany, France and elsewhere.

The first evening that Lorena and Gian Andrea went to the piazza in 2015 to meet with the arriving migrants, it was only the two of them "with a small trolley of medications, mostly to treat people's foot problems," said Lorena.

Before long, other volunteers from Italy and in some cases from abroad began showing up. By 2019, the couple had set up a group, Linea d'Ombra, to organize volunteers and coordinate aid for migrants in Trieste and along the Balkan route. The group describes itself as "political rather than humanitarian."

Lorena explained: "We see this work as a political commitment rather than a humanitarian one. We don't limit ourselves to providing humanitarian assistance. We also produce reports and undertake advocacy. We want to address the causes that lead to suffering. Migration is a key issue of our time, and we support people's right to move from one territory to another."

Funded solely by private donors, the group also relies on help from scout groups, associations, parishes, and private individuals from across Italy.

The name Linea d'Ombra, Lorena explained, is taken from Joseph Conrad's 1917 novella, *The Shadow-Line,* about a young sea captain who, on his first command, makes a life-threatening journey, facing numerous obstacles, including the hostility of the open ocean.

"The refugees on the Balkan route are on the threshold between shadow and light, on the border between death and survival," she said.

Lorena, Gian Andrea, and others from their group have traveled to Balkan countries, including Bosnia, Serbia, and Bulgaria, to better understand what the migrants have been through before they arrive in Trieste and to provide financial support to similar organizations.

In 2018, Gian Andrea was taking photos of Lorena tending to a refugee's feet for their social media platforms. One image, to their surprise, went viral, touching a nerve in people across Italy and beyond.

"[The photo] shook the souls of a lot of people," said Lorena. "Everybody saw it from a different angle. For me, it's a political act; for others, it had a religious meaning. Some saw it as a humanitarian message."

For many, the image simply represented care and the power of human touch. In Christian culture, washing someone's feet is an act of forgiveness and compassion. It features in all four Gospels that recount Jesus's life in the New Testament. In the most famous incident, Jesus interrupts his last meal with his disciples on the evening before his crucifixion, hours before he is arrested. According to the Gospel of John, this is what transpires:

> [Jesus] rose from supper and took off his outer garments. He took a towel and tied it around his waist. Then he poured water into a basin and

> began to wash the disciples' feet and dry them with the towel around his waist. So when he had washed their feet [and] put his garments back on and reclined at table again, he said to them, "Do you realize what I have done for you? You call me 'teacher' and 'master,' and rightly so, for indeed I am. If I, therefore, the master and teacher, have washed your feet, you ought to wash one another's feet. I have given you a model to follow, so that as I have done for you, you should also do."

The story is commemorated throughout Italy and in the rest of the Christian world as a lesson in humility. On Holy Thursday, in the week leading up to Easter Sunday, parishes in churches all over the world reenact Jesus's washing of the feet. Despite a decline in religious observance and church attendance across western Europe, the act continues to hold profound symbolic meaning.

"For me, tending to someone's feet is just natural. I've been doing it for so long, I don't even really think about it or pay much attention to the fact that I'm touching a stranger's feet," said Lorena.

Reactions to the image led Lorena to reflect more deeply on the practice. The sister of a man who disappeared during the war in Syria in 2013 wrote her a letter, saying, "You are touching the lowest part of the body, but at the same time you are touching the part that sustains the whole body, our feet."

"So I realized that when I am touching someone's feet, I'm not only touching them physically, I'm touching their soul at the same time," observed Lorena. "Every line and wrinkle I see represents the scars and violence they have endured on their journey."

For Gian Andrea, caring for a migrant's feet goes beyond simple words that you can say to someone to reassure them that they are a human being: "It crosses the abyss that exists between the other person and me."

I met Lorena and Gian Andrea in their apartment in July 2025. Sunlight streamed through the windows onto walls that were lined with new and old books, a library of political history and ideas. A pile of their grandchildren's toys was neatly stacked in a corner near the front door. As one might expect from a former psychotherapist and a former philosophy teacher who have both published books in their fields, our discussion about their motivation to do good was long and thoughtful.

Lorena showed me a book by Genevieve Vaughan, *Le radici materne dell'economia del dono* (*The Maternal Roots of the Gift Economy*). Over the last fifty years, Vaughan and others have emphasized the importance of unilateral gift-giving in forming the foundation of a compassionate society. It rejects traditional ideas of exchange and competition or of expecting anything in return for giving gifts.

"We call it the practice of caring," says Lorena.

Even so, there's no doubt working with migrants has given Lorena and Gian Andrea a great deal in return. Lorena said it has given her a certain confidence and an increased capacity to think positively about other people.

"[It's] always good to think well of others," said Lorena. "It's *la pratica dell'amore,* the practice of love. What Gian Andrea and I now do together, we are no longer normal human beings, living a normal life. . . . We have created these new layers in our lives," she said.

When I asked what had led them to dedicate their lives to helping migrants, the couple pointed to many influences. For Lorena, perhaps the most profound was her mother, whom she described as "the strong root of my existence." As she was explaining this, she handed me a book that she herself wrote, *Tutte le anime del mio corpo: Diario di una giovane partigiana (1943–1945)—All the Souls of My Body: Diary of a Young Partisan (1943–1945)*—an account of her late mother, Maria Antonietta Moro, who fought against the Nazis.

The book draws on her mother's wartime diaries and on letters she exchanged with Lorena's future father, the partisan commander Ardito "Ario" Fornasir. Lorena discovered these materials only in 2009, after her mother's death.

Lorena told me that she always knew of her mother's "strength, her courage, her love of life, her care, her attraction to the mystery surrounding a sunrise, a sunset, a drop of dew," but the discovery of the diaries and letters revealed a version of Antonietta that Lorena had never seen.

"I lived with my mother for a whole lifetime without knowing her completely," Lorena wrote in the book.

Antonietta Moro worked as a nurse, passing information she gleaned from German soldiers on to the partisans. Initially involved with the Yugoslavian anti-fascist groups, she later joined the resistance in Italy. She wrote her diary after being forced into hiding near the end of the war, and it remained undiscovered for six decades. The letters Lorena found show her mother's passion, idealism, and strength. In one letter, dated April 7, 1945, Ario, writes to Antonietta, "They tell me you're organizing some comrades. And this makes me angry because by doing so you are exposing yourself unnecessarily in a job that is not yours and that you cannot do well."

In the book, Lorena reflected on the way her parents influenced her political activism: "During those years of strikes and union struggles in the mid-1950s, family life was, for my parents, a communal space where individual well-being was only achieved through social struggle. With her singular approach of never backing down in the face of obstacles, my mother introduced me to real life.... She showed me we must give something of ourselves in order to reach others."

Lorena recalled that when the police were deployed against workers' marches, which were led by her father, "my mother put stones and pebbles in the palms of my sister's and my hands to throw at the riot police. Crouching on our backs in the ditch surrounding the appliance factory, we breathed in the wind of rebellion and freedom that marked our entry into civil society. . . . I don't remember actually throwing those stones at the riot police charging the union marchers. What I do remember is feeling proud of my father."

Like Lorena, Gian Andrea grew up surrounded by the energy of political activism. He recalled that when he was teaching, back in the 1960s and 1970s, "students didn't just sit back and take in the information they were given; they acted on their own opinions, sometimes by going to the streets. This is what formed my political background."

Lorena and Gian Andrea's concern about migration extends far beyond the streets of Trieste and the countries along the Balkan route. Gian Andrea spoke about climate change forcing more and more people from some countries as rising temperatures and shifts in rainfall destroy livelihoods. According to the World Bank, climate-related factors in sub-Saharan Africa, South Asia, Latin America, and other regions are increasingly harmful.

"[We are] on the brink of a humanitarian crisis. We need to find a different way to manage the planet and how to share it," he said.

Turning to the crisis in Gaza, he noted that Israel's atrocities have highlighted the urgent need for work that defends human rights.

"Now there is a genocide on TV. We need to wake up and just not give in to this law of the jungle, where the strongest win. We have to find a way to stop this extreme violence," he said. "Some people are protesting, yes, but it's not enough."

Musing on what US President Donald Trump prioritizes and cares about, Gian Andrea said, "Money is what matters. Israel, and behind them the United States, treat Palestinians as packages to move from one place to another, to build a beautiful resort in Gaza and transform it into a paradise."

Although most evenings, Lorena and Gian Andrea are now joined in the Trieste piazza by other helpers, some local and some from far away, Gian Andrea sees them as a "minority" of those who could help. He has been encouraging more people, especially the younger generation, to get involved. In talks he gives to scouts, and to school and university students, he has emphasized that they should go beyond the self-satisfaction of giving a vulnerable person food and water, to understand what leads people to flee countries in the first place, "no matter what the root causes of the violence are."

The former philosophy teacher worries that the revolution in communication has not contributed to building this understanding.

"In fact, it's made things worse," he asserted. "People look at their phones, watch a video of what's happening in Gaza, and then turn on the TV to watch a football match. People have become indifferent to what they are watching, as if this is now normal, like life is just a bit of film to be glanced at and then discarded."

Becoming indifferent is not an option for Gian Andrea.

"I continue doing what I have to do because I want to give sense and meaning to my life," he said. "As long as I breathe, I will continue doing that. Even if what's happening out in the world is not giving me any optimism."

Lorena and Gian Andrea's daily acts of kindness have angered some locals over the years, including the authorities. At 5:00 a.m. on February 23, 2021, five police officers banged on the door of their apartment.

"They came in, they had a warrant, and they sort of hysterically started to search the house, looking in drawers and taking Gian Andrea's laptop and computer," said Lorena. "They took mine, too, but I told them I had a hearing at the court that day, and I can't do that if you take my phone and laptop."

For two years before the raid, Lorena had been an honorary judge in Trieste's juvenile courts, contacting social services, interviewing people, and assessing families' suitability for adopting children. She had passed an exam qualifying her for a role advising another judge how to make the most appropriate decisions for all those involved.

That morning, the officers took Gian Andrea to the police station and accused him of illegally harboring people. They took his mug shot and sent him home. Lorena, meanwhile, went to the court as planned, only to find when she arrived at the appointed courtroom, that she had been removed from her case with the hearing that day, as well as all other cases.

"They didn't ask me to resign; they didn't write to me to tell me what was happening; they didn't tell me I was dismissed," she said. "From that day, they just took me off all the cases, all the interviews. I wrote to them asking what had happened, and they just never responded. It was really devastating."

The police's case against the couple referred to an incident two years before, when Gian Andrea and Lorena had let a migrant family of Kurds from Iran with two young children stay in their home for two nights when they had nowhere else to go. This was somehow now a crime.

"We couldn't leave them out on the street," said Gian Andrea.

Because of Lorena's ties as an honorary judge in the Trieste court system, the case was moved to the jurisdiction of Bologna to be heard. Soon after, the charges were dropped without any hearing for "a lack of evidence," much to the couple's irritation.

"We wanted our day in court," said Lorena.

She and Gian Andrea thought a court hearing would be beneficial, in that it might encourage others to open their doors to migrants.

"We wanted there to be a public hearing about what we had done, so more people could hear about our work," Lorena said, "but after they came into our home and searched it, they denied us that chance."

Gian Andrea says the investigation was part of a repressive agenda to target people who work with migrants, that it was about more than him and Lorena as individuals, that it was a warning to others about the consequences of helping people.

Although helping people each day has given them a great sense of purpose, the pair admitted that it has also cast a shadow on their lives. Taking a vacation—something they used to enjoy doing every year—they now see as a selfish luxury. The very idea of it makes them feel guilty.

Trieste's coastline is celebrated for its dramatic landscapes and sparkling harbor, but Lorena can no longer look at the sea without thinking of death.

"How can we enjoy the sea when we know it is full of bodies floating; nobody is rescuing them, or even bringing them back to their loved ones to grieve properly?" Lorena asked. "How can I enjoy any of that anymore when I know the reality, when I know the truth of what's happening in the middle of that sea? How can I go to Croatia on vacation, knowing what people on the Balkan route are experiencing there?"

Lorena said she learned from her mother the value of "standing in the face of problems and finding the strength not to give in to indifference, individualism, the destructiveness of the banality of evil." But taking a stand every day can be exhausting. The couple hasn't had a holiday since that day in 2015.

One day, she asked her husband, "What on earth are we doing? Are we crazy people to keep going to the piazza every night?"

Gian Andrea reminded her that their work helping migrants is now inescapably their life's meaning. "We are like thieves. Every night, we go outside and steal a little bit of the sense of life. We take what we need to be alive today," he said.

This reply, Lorena said, gave her "some peace inside" and helped her to continue. "That and our continual support for each other. We realized that it doesn't make sense to enjoy life while there is so much suffering around us."

"Life today isn't about living," said Gian Andrea. "By acting together with migrants, we try in whatever way we can to transform mere survival into solidarity."

CHAPTER 8

FIDELMA O'KANE AND CORMAC MCALEER, NORTHERN IRELAND

The Sperrin Mountains, Northern Ireland's largest mountain range, is internationally known for its natural reservoirs, clear rivers, ancient peatlands, and deep valleys. People travel from afar to visit the area, which has long been considered one of Ireland's great natural treasures.

Cormac McAleer and his wife, Fidelma O'Kane, both grew up nearby and have spent most of their lives in Northern Ireland. They were teenagers when the Northern Ireland conflict (1969–1998) began and experienced those years in areas marked by fear and extreme violence. Military checkpoints were common, and news of local bombings and shootings were part of everyday life. Although the conflict still shapes the history of where they live, a greater sense of normalcy has settled onto the community.

When I sat with them at their kitchen table in their house, set along a quiet rural lane, Fidelma explained how in 2013 they heard of plans for a gold mining venture in the area.

"I thought the government would never allow this," she said. "I was naive, really."

There were many reasons Cormac and Fidelma believed mining would never go ahead in the Sperrins. The region had been recognized as an area of outstanding natural beauty since 1968, and it contains two rivers that are Special Areas of Conservation, protected zones created under EU law.

Then, in December 2014, Fidelma recalled, "one of our neighbors stopped by and said if you go over to the mining company office, you can get a Christmas hamper for free. She said you just go in, sign your name, and you get a hamper. And I thought, 'Uh-oh, there's no such thing as a free hamper.'"

In the coming months, as Cormac and Fidelma heard more about the proposed mine and its likely impact on the local land, their concerns grew. And so, in June 2015, they organized a meeting at the local Greencastle Community Centre, near where they lived, for locals and others to share what they knew about the venture. About twenty people showed up. Those invited to speak included Geoffrey Simpson, an antiques expert and auctioneer from the nearby town of Omagh; James Orr, from the environmental NGO Friends of the Earth; and Eamonn McCann, a gifted orator and veteran civil rights leader from Derry.

Their area had been at the center of the peaceful civil rights marches in the late 1960s, which sought to end discrimination against Catholics on issues such as the allocation of housing and voting rights. As a seventeen-year-old boy, Cormac had joined McCann and many others on some of the earliest civil rights marches in Northern Ireland, including the very first, in August 1968. The movement in Northern Ireland was partly inspired by the US civil rights protests of the 1960s. Irish protesters chanted the same slogans and sang "We Shall Overcome" and other songs borrowed from the US movement. It's an issue I've researched and written about extensively. While the US civil rights movement achieved some success in terms of voting rights and desegregation, attempted reforms by authorities in Northern Ireland were too little and too late, and the popular energy for peaceful change in the late 1960s was stifled in the decades of strife that followed.

The Northern Ireland conflict, often understatedly called "the Troubles," entailed an extraordinary level of violence. Thousands of people were killed by Irish republican armed groups, who wanted to break away from British rule; by British loyalist paramilitary groups, who wanted to maintain British rule; and by the UK security forces. An increasing amount of evidence is emerging of widespread collusion by the British State with paramilitary organizations, its paid agents committing crimes, including murder, with impunity.

Overall, an estimated 3,720 people were killed and 47,541 were injured in the Northern Ireland conflict. About 54 percent of those killed and 68 percent of those injured were civilians. Many were killed or wounded in sectarian attacks for being Catholics or for being Protestants. Northern Ireland's population during those years was just over 1.5 million people.

By the time Cormac and Fidelma and their group met in the bar of the community center that night in June 2015, the widespread violence had ended only seventeen years earlier, not a long time in the history of the community or in local memory. But that evening, the conversation was about the mine, with a mix of Catholics and Protestants showing up. They exchanged what they knew about the project and its potential impact on the area. James Orr from Friends of the Earth gave a PowerPoint presentation with pictures of the freshwater pearl mussel, Ireland's only endangered species.

"I'd never seen pictures of them before and didn't know they can live to be one hundred and forty years old," said Fidelma.

"It's a sign of clear, clean water if you have these mussels. They latch onto the gills of spawning salmon. Then they bury themselves in the clean sand or gravel at the bottom of the river and filter the water. I was amazed by all this; it was all news to me. We learned back in 2014 that the authorities had given the mining company a three-year license for an exploration tunnel but that the license had forty-four conditions, including that they had to restore the site to its original condition. That night we resolved we would organize a campaign group and call ourselves Save Our Sperrins."

Since then, the group has worked to warn the public and the government about the potential dangers of the mining project. They say that operations will release heavy metals into two protected rivers, threatening aquatic life, such as the freshwater pearl mussels, salmon, trout, and otters. They also warn that the air will be contaminated by fine dust from mine waste containing heavy metals, by radon gas released from underground mining, by the twice-daily explosions every day of the year, and by diesel fumes from the millions of liters of fuel expected to be used on site each year for at least two decades.

Campaigners emphasize that protecting the Sperrins is about protecting Ireland's future.

"The mountains support farming, ecotourism, and livelihoods that depend on the land being healthy and intact. And let's not forget the peatlands," said Marella Fyffe, chairperson of Save Our Sperrins. "These aren't just patches of wet ground. They're nature's way of storing carbon—a frontline defense against climate change, so important in the world today."

There is obvious local pride taken in the countryside, with a palpable connection to the past.

"The Sperrins hold stories that go back thousands of years," said Fyffe. "They connect us to the people who came before us. They're more than just a landscape. They're a link to our shared past. Really, a link to Ireland's soul. They remind us of who we are and what we value."

A painted stone at the side of one of the roads in the area simply says "Cherish the Land." Half-hidden on one of the mountainsides sits a Mass rock that was used as an altar to celebrate outdoor Catholic Masses during the sixteenth, seventeenth, and eighteenth centuries, when practicing Catholicism was outlawed under English rule. During these years of intense persecution, when priests found holding services were hunted down and executed, secret Catholic Masses were held around such flat-topped slabs in remote places offering natural concealment. They remain powerful symbols of local resistance and resilience.

Time ticks differently here—some things barely change over generations. Tractors crawl along the narrow laneways, farm dogs still run out to bark at passing traffic, and sheep cling to the hilly fields, daubed with red or blue dye to show who owns them.

About a mile from the Greencastle Community Centre on Mullydoo Road, a loudly babbling stream leads down through a field to the ancient Aghascrebagh Ogham Stone. The square gray upright slab is about five feet high and two feet wide. An inscription dates it to around 500 C.E., during the Iron Age. Like the few ancient ogham stones across Ireland, the writing on it is made up of horizontal lines, each about six inches long, forming a shape like a ladder. The lines, marked on one corner and read from the bottom up, translate as "DOTETTO MAQI MAGLANI"—Dotetto son of Maglani—and link two male names. The stone is believed to be a burial marker.

Local legend has it there is an underground tunnel extending away from the stone, but often such stories are best left unexplored. The explanatory note posted next to the slab says many locals "will not touch such features on their land in fear of some repercussions by the fairies." It's said a former landowner who lived in the now ruined cottage close by decided he wanted to remove the ogham stone and began to dig around it. However, bad fortune followed. No sooner had he started work than groundwater began to rise in the barn, bringing havoc to his buildings and animals. When the farmer decided to stop the digging work, the water receded as quickly as it had started and normality returned to his farm.

Other local tales passed down through the centuries tell of another landowner, a giant of a man, who was tied to the stone for some misdemeanor and guarded there by twelve strong men. But the landowner tore loose from his restraints and killed all the guards, who tradition says were buried in the graveyard across the road. The story goes on to say that the landowner himself is buried under the ogham stone.

The stone was here hundreds of years before the English invaded and was probably put up around the time of Saint Patrick, who is credited with bringing Christianity to Ireland. The nearby village church, named after the saint, is small. Graves cluster tightly around three of its sides. Some date back to the 1860s. "Here we speak of life beyond life and life after death," reads the inscription at the entrance. The cemetery offers clues to a complicated local history, but in many ways it's a typical Irish parish graveyard, with hundreds of gravestones reflecting wealth, poverty, infant deaths, war, and emigration. Some names on the gravestones are in English, some Irish, some both. There are single plots, some neglected, and large family gravesites holding dozens of relatives together in their embrace.

One family grave has a dark square slab with gold lettering lying on shiny black gravel covering the plot. A Kathleen O'Hagan is buried here. Her name is also in Irish—Caitlín Ó hÁgáin. It says starkly in both languages:

> Dedicated Wife & Mother
> Brutally Murdered by British Agents
> On 7th August 1994
> Fondly Remembered by the People of the Area

Kathleen O'Hagan and her family were close neighbors of Cormac and Fidelma. A thirty-eight-year-old mother of five children, Kathleen was seven months pregnant that Sunday night when she was shot dead in front of her children, who ranged in age from fifteen months to eight years old. Kathleen's husband, Paddy, who was believed to have been the intended target, was away when the gunmen entered their bedroom and fired more than a dozen bullets at Kathleen.

The Ulster Volunteer Force, a Loyalist paramilitary group, later claimed the murder. The group was known for sectarian attacks against Catholics and those it suspected of supporting the Irish Republican Army. The family claimed the attack followed years of harassment by the police and the British Army, and that, not long before Kathleen's murder, security forces had sealed off their home for four days, wrecking it and digging up the surrounding land.

"We remember that night so clearly," said Cormac. "A beautiful summer evening. We were driving past their house, and I said to Fidelma how well it was looking after the family had put everything back to normal after it had been dug up."

Fidelma recalled, "We were on our way to a Frances Black concert in Omagh that night when we passed the house. And then we got the call the next morning. I'll never forget it. It was so terrible."

As elsewhere in Northern Ireland, many villages in the area still display British or Irish flags, clearly signaling their allegiances—orange symbols or British flags generally mark Protestant areas, while green symbols or Irish flags signal Catholic communities. The conflict inevitably played a major part in the lives of everyone in the area.

In 1971, when Fidelma was sixteen, she went for her summer holidays to work as a housekeeper for her mother's brother, the parish priest in Strabane, less than twenty miles from her home.

The early 1970s were among the most brutally violent years of the conflict. Fidelma recalled accompanying her uncle one August afternoon when he was called to the scene of a shooting in the town. Eamonn McDevitt, a twenty-eight-year-old deaf and mute man, had been shot by a British soldier.

"I remember we got there and the poor man was lying in the road, dead," said Fidelma. "It was a terrible shock. I'd never seen anything like that, but those days were awful, awful. It was really dangerous. Every week, there were more people being killed."

Soon after, Fidelma started at Queen's University in Belfast, studying social sciences. Much of the city was a dangerous patchwork of sectarian neighborhoods. Bombings and shootings were an everyday hazard, as the conflict defined almost every aspect of normal life. The university was one of the few places where Protestants and Catholics met socially.

One Sunday afternoon, when Fidelma was eighteen, she went to visit a friend in her class who was at the city's Royal Victoria Hospital, a mile and a half from the university. The thirty-minute walk from the university required walking along the Donegall Road through a Protestant neighborhood.

"It so happens this friend was a Protestant girl, and I went to see her with another girl, a Catholic. A gang of young men came out of a side street and stopped us and asked where we were from. My friend said she was from Derry," recalled Fidelma, covering her face with her hand at the memory. Saying "Derry" was an immediate tell, revealing that her friend was a Catholic, because Protestants called the city Londonderry.

"Oh, God, they grabbed us, and they pulled us down to the ground," continued Fidelma. "There had been a bonfire on the side of the street, and they started grabbing ashes and charcoal from it with their hands, shoveling it into our mouths. We were gagging, and I was terrified, and—I don't know how I found the strength, from the fear, I suppose—I managed to force myself up, and I ran.

My friend struggled and got away, too. A wee woman, living on a Protestant street, saw what was happening and opened her door and she said, 'Come in here, you'll be all right in here, girls,' and we escaped into her house for a while. Thank God for that woman; we were really afraid."

In 1979, Fidelma and Cormac volunteered with Mother Teresa's Missionaries of Charity in India, spending weeks working in a home for the dying, then at an orphanage in Calcutta, and finally at a home for people with leprosy.

"It was really tough," said Fidelma. "People were dying in the streets, and conditions in the orphanage and the other places were just terrible. Three kids are standing on a cot, just rocking and banging their heads against a wall. There were hundreds of children, and they'd all be wanting your attention. It was really hard. We weren't used to anything like that, nobody's used to that, that's not normal. I suppose that experience was always in my head. I mean, you come back and it makes you appreciate what you have."

When they returned home, Fidelma continued to take on tough jobs, working as a social worker on cases involving sexual and physical abuse of children.

"Often I felt you couldn't do right for doing wrong. If you remove a child from his parents, it was traumatic for the child," she recalled. "And no matter how bad the parents were to them, that child often still loved them. I've been in court when a child has to be separated from their parents because of the awful things they've done to the child, and then in the court, you see the child run to the parents. I often thought what was the right thing to do? You know, it was really difficult."

The work drained Fidelma mentally and emotionally.

"I had four young children," she said, "and I was coming home, telling my boys just to be quiet. I'd say to Cormac: 'I have nothing to give my own children because I'm dealing with so much at work.'"

Fidelma finally left social work after fifteen years, but the couple stayed engaged with world affairs. In the mid- to late 1980s, they took their young children to Dublin to join protests against the racist South African apartheid regime. A teacher at their sons' primary school joked to Fidelma how impressed she was with the caliber of their family's friends: "Your boys told me you sent a Christmas card to Nelson Mandela in prison."

Nevertheless, taking on a gold mine was a very different prospect than working for Mother Teresa, writing letters to Mandela, or anything else Fidelma and Cormac had experienced during the years of conflict in Northern Ireland. Dalradian, the mining company, had in fact been working on a site in nearby Gortin since 2009, years before the 2015 community center meeting. The area is believed to contain significant gold, silver, copper, and other mineral deposits. The company claimed the site could produce one hundred metric tons of gold, forty-eight metric tons of silver, and fifteen thousand metric tons of copper over a twenty- to twenty-five-year span. Even though Dalradian promised jobs and investment with the mining project, more than fifty thousand objections have been lodged against granting the company planning permission for a gold mine. Local opposition remains fierce.

"The jobs are temporary, and the damage is permanent," said Fidelma.

Fidelma, Cormac, and other locals have spent years wrangling with local authorities about the mining company's proposals, learning how the permissions process works in terms of granting prospective mining licenses to corporations, what can be done to object, and what forms of legal recourse are open to the community.

"We're not lawyers, and we didn't ever expect to find ourselves filing planning objections, organizing representation at public inquiries, or facing down multinational mining companies," said Fidelma. But going through the mine's planning application taught her a lot. "It taught me to read fast and to understand the technical language used. For instance, the 2017 planning application was ten thousand pages long, the 2019 First Addendum was fifteen thousand pages, and the 2020 Second Addendum twenty thousand pages. There was a lot to understand."

In 2017, the government's Environment Agency granted Dalradian a Discharge Consent, allowing the company to flush water containing nine heavy metals, including arsenic, mercury, cadmium, chromium, zinc, and lead, into the Owenkillew River, where the freshwater pearl mussels live. The decision was made at the end of the year, and the only way to challenge it was to take it to a judicial review at the court, but there was a tight deadline to lodge an objection.

"It was December, and Cormac had gone away to visit a friend who'd retired in Cyprus," recalled Fidelma, "so I texted him: 'I'm thinking of requesting a judicial review, what do you think?' And he said, 'Do what you want because you'll do it anyway. . . .'"

Fidelma had no idea how to go about presenting her case at the judicial review at the High Court in Belfast, so she found a textbook, *Judicial Review in Northern Ireland,* by Gordon Anthony, to help. The four-hundred-page law book outlined how the procedure works, relevant case law, principles and practice, and various other legal analyses.

"I read it from cover to cover and made thorough notes," said Fidelma. "When I went to the court, I was given an hour to speak, and it was like an out-of-body experience; I was so nervous. There were two bottles of water in front of me, so after every point I made, I took a sip to try to stay calm and slow down. Inside, I was thinking, 'I can't believe I'm up here in the High Court in Belfast and I'm talking like I know something,' but after a while, I felt myself getting stronger. I'd done my homework, and I spoke for an hour and a quarter."

At the end of her speech, Justice Siobhan Keegan, the judge, asked Fidelma if she had a background in law.

"And I said no, no, I read a book. I said a really good book, *Judicial Review in Northern Ireland,* by Gordon Anthony, and I just followed it very carefully. And Justice Keegan was smiling, and she said, 'Do you know that Mr. Anthony is in the court?' And I said no, and she pointed and said, 'There he is, he's one of Dalradian's barristers.' Well, I always say, the ground will never open and swallow me if it didn't do it that day."

After twenty-three months of legal proceedings, Fidelma won the case, and the permission to grant the dumping of metals was quashed. She said she asked if Gordon Anthony would sign her copy of his book for her, but he declined.

Alongside the victories, there have been darker days as well.

One afternoon in June 2019, a car pulled up outside Fidelma and Cormac's house, and two police officers in uniform stepped out.

"A man and a woman," recalled Fidelma. "We let them in, and the woman said how much she liked our kitchen. I was telling her how we renovated it, and it was all very friendly, and then the policeman cleared his throat and said, 'The reason we are here is to tell you there is a credible death threat against Cormac. Our sergeant asked us to deliver the message. All we're telling you is there's a credible death threat against you, and we would advise you to take precautions, and we have a booklet here we can give you about precautions.'"

Fidelma remembered it as a surreal moment: "We were just shocked. We asked what more could they tell us. Was the threat made on a phone call, in a letter, or what? Was it an individual? Was it an organization? And the officer said: 'We can't tell you anything else. We're delivering the message from our sergeant.' And away they went. I just stood there with my mouth open."

The couple never learned any more about who was behind the threat, although Fidelma said two other men who also received death threats were part of the Save Our Sperrins campaign. During the Troubles, the threat of violence was ever-present, and it left the Sperrins community painfully aware of how power can be abused and the local community treated as disposable. Some see the opposition to the Dalradian mining project as part of Ireland's historical resistance to outside forces that seek to dictate the fate of the land with no regard for those who live on it. But the campaign is also crucially different from the Troubles.

"It is organizing the two sides, Catholics and Protestants—we have support from both communities," said Fidelma. "This isn't about orange or green because pollution doesn't differentiate."

Cormac and Fidelma showed me around the mountainside where a protest camp, the Greencastle People's Office (GPO), had been set up in February 2018. The abbreviation "GPO" has great resonance in Ireland as letters symbolic of resistance, because Ireland's 1916 revolution started in Dublin's General Post Office, often referred to by its GPO initials. Two small caravans and some tables set beside them outside were empty in the cold of the winter when I visited, but in the warmer months the spot is a hub of local activity against the mine, attracting people from across the country and beyond. The caravans are covered in slogans, such as *Fáilte* (Irish for "welcome"); "Greencastle GPO"; "We are not afraid"; "This is our land, this is our home, we will die for it"; "No to mining in Greencastle"; and "Health before gold."

"We've had people here supporting us from Romania, Brazil, Peru, Mexico, and India," said Cormac. "And Native American, Lakota."

There was a BBC Northern Ireland Spotlight TV documentary about the mining project, shown in October 2021. They had gone to Brazil to show what the company had done there.

"It [the documentary] really helped us understand more about how these things work. It brought us a lot of support, too," Cormac said.

Pointing out the ancient Mass rock on the mountain and a nearby pasture where cattle graze, Cormac shared that the milk farmer who works the land feared that the grass the cows would eat would be contaminated and the milk rendered useless. He showed me an adjacent field where, in January 2019, he took the extraordinary step of tying himself to a drilling rig to stop the mining. Dressed like a mining company employee in a high-visibility yellow jacket and a white construction worker's helmet, Cormac managed to get access to the rig and remain there from noon until 8:00 p.m.

"I got into the field and had a chain padlocked around my waist, tying me to the rig," recalled Cormac. "The company called the cops at once, and they came and asked me what it was about. It stopped them working for a bit."

Fidelma laughed, remembering that protest: "I was bringing soup and sandwiches to [Cormac], but he was on the other side of an eight-foot fence, and I thought, 'How am I ever going to get over that?' So when the cops weren't looking, I crawled underneath it." Cormac's protest generated more publicity for the campaign.

Although Cormac was not arrested or charged with trespassing for that incident, he has been summoned to the police station, taken to court several times for his protests, and twice served with official cautions.

While the mining company has been able to push on with some exploratory work, full planning permission for its application for large-scale mining is still under review. The local struggle against it continues. At the same time, Fidelma and Cormac are aware of neighbors who don't feel they can publicly support the campaign.

"Yes, there are people who just sit back to let us and the others do it, but there are pressures on young people, too. They're watching out for their jobs, their mortgages, and paying a fortune for childcare. They're caught in the system. But around here, I'd say 95 percent of the locals are behind us," said Cormac.

In 2019, Emmet McAleer, one of the couple's sons, successfully ran for a seat on the local council as an independent to raise issues about the mining. Along with others from the Save Our Sperrins Campaign, Fidelma and Cormac have also visited London twice—in 2021 and 2025—to advocate against the mine.

"From the outside, it might look like a local dispute," one member of Save Our Sperrins said. "We've come to understand that what we're part of is something much bigger: a front line in the global fight for climate justice and human rights."

The campaign has drawn support—and criticism—from strong international voices. United Nations Special Rapporteur for Human Rights Defenders Mary Lawlor spoke at a 2025 event to mark the tenth anniversary of the campaign, noting that across the world protecting the environment is often a very dangerous activity.

The campaign said Mary Lawlor's support brought "not just international recognition, but dignity. She reminded us that the right to defend your land is . . . a right enshrined in international law. Her presence gave weight to what we've always known: Defending the earth is defending human rights." Protestors have noted, "What started as a quiet planning application has become a long, exhausting, and deeply personal struggle—not just for our environment, but for our rights, our peace of mind, and the future of our communities."

As of early 2026, Dalradian still holds a live application to mine gold in the Sperrin Mountains. They await a decision from the Northern Ireland authorities—and they have reason to be hopeful. In 2025, four members of the US Congress reportedly complained about the decade of delays to the mining project and blamed the protesters for "yet again" holding up the venture. Their public criticism was widely seen as a message to the Northern Ireland authorities to grant permission for the project to go ahead.

A few months later, US Ambassador to the United Kingdom Warren Stephens also suggested in a speech that "unnecessary delays" over an application for further mining were "harming" Northern Ireland's reputation. "Bureaucracy must not become a barrier to progress. You cannot expect a US company to make a major investment here if they cannot be certain when they will get an answer from planning authorities," Stephens said.

More than fifty years ago, civil rights marchers in Northern Ireland here looked to Dr. Martin Luther King Jr. and other American leaders for inspiration, and today's protesters similarly draw on US voices to guide their activism. A pamphlet produced by the Save Our Sperrins campaign even quotes JFK—no further identification is needed, as everyone in Northern Ireland knows who President John F. Kennedy was—saying, "One person can make a difference, and everyone should try." The pamphlet also quotes a Native American Cree as saying: "When all the trees have been cut down, when all the animals have been hunted, when all the waters are polluted, when all the air is unsafe to breathe, only then will you discover you cannot eat money."

The campaign has expressed real frustration that local amateurs have been left to do the work of the authorities. "Why is environmental jurisprudence left to farmers, grandmothers, and teachers working unpaid late into the night just to uphold the most basic rights to clean water, fresh air, and a livable climate?" protestors ask in a pamphlet.

Cormac and Fidelma had to buy a new, larger kitchen table to work on as their piles of research and campaign papers kept growing and spilling onto the floor. They have no intention of stopping their work against the mine.

"All this campaigning is a big enough job for now," Fidelma said. "But we're forever finding more documents to read, and we're learning from people resisting gold mining around the globe. We haven't found one good news story about it yet, but we are optimistic about stopping Dalradian's gold mining application if common sense is to prevail. Who could argue against the need to keep the water and air clean and the land unpolluted for the health of future generations in the Sperrins? Money or gold can't buy health."

Now in their second decade of this fight, Fidelma and Cormac have nine grandchildren and are aware of what they're sacrificing.

"Sometimes I think with all this work on the campaign, we're losing out on time with them," said Fidelma. "But we're doing it for their future, we're doing it for them, so they will have clean water, fresh air, beautiful scenery, and unpolluted soil to enjoy."

CHAPTER 9

THE ATLAS OF HATE ACTIVISTS, POLAND

Poland has long had a contentious and repressive record on sexual rights. Though not a crime in Poland before the Nazi invasion in 1939, homosexuality was largely a taboo subject and disapproved of by much of society. Following the invasion, the new German occupiers made homosexuality illegal and subject to severe reprisals. After the Second World War, in both Soviet-dominated Poland and under Poland's new pro-Western democracy, the rights of sexual identity have remained a consistently tense political issue.

The Catholic Church has been a steadfast and powerful anti-LGBTQ+ force, and the issue has been regularly exploited by political figures on the right. Poland's conservative Law and Justice Party, which led the government for eight years between 2015 and 2023, consistently made homophobia a central electoral theme. Although Poland has been a member of the European Union (EU) since 2004, local and national politicians have criticized what they claim is excessive interference by the EU, pushing a permissive liberal social agenda onto the country. Today, same-sex marriage is still illegal in Poland, as it is in five other EU countries.

In April 2018, the leader of the Law and Justice Party, Jarosław Kaczyński, declared during a local election campaign that "no homosexual marriages will occur; we will wait peacefully for the European Union countries to sober up." Six months later, the mayor of Lublin banned an Equality March five days before it was supposed to take place. Although the courts ordered the ban to be lifted, more local politicians began attacking LGBTQ+ rights.

At the end of March 2019, councilors in Świdnica County in the heart of Poland adopted a declaration: "Świdnica County Free from LGBT Ideology." Although the resolution had no legal power, the message was still a powerful gesture promoting discrimination and hostility toward LGBTQ+ people. The idea took flight across Poland, and in the following months more than one hundred cities and municipalities adopted similar "LGBT-free zone" declarations, covering one-third of the entire country. Dozens of these communities also signed a homophobic "Local Government Charter of Family Rights" initiated by the ultraconservative, Catholic Ordo Iuris, Institute for Legal Culture. The charter encouraged councils to recognize only heterosexual couples as families.

Fueled by these resolutions, fear and hatred spread across Poland throughout 2019. In the central-western city of Gniezno, a car drove around displaying a banner that read "What the LGBT lobby wants to teach kids: Masturbation; consenting to sex; first sexual experiences and orgasms. Stop pedophilia." Similar messages were later seen on other cars and trucks throughout the country. The resolutions had devastating effects on LGBTQ+ people living in these areas. A study published in 2025 found suicide rates had risen 16 percent in the zones, particularly among teenagers and middle-aged people, driven by the intensifying stigma.

In June 2019, the mayor of Rzeszów attempted to ban the city's scheduled Equality March, but the decision was overturned by a court, and the march went ahead under heavy police protection. When a similar march took place in the eastern city of Białystok the following month, marchers were violently attacked by anti-LGBTQ+ demonstrators.

Horrified at what was unfolding, a small group of friends began messaging on WhatsApp, trying to figure out what could be done. Part of the problem was keeping track of all the municipalities passing these harmful resolutions and explaining the extent of the hostility.

In 2019, Kuba Gawron was in his mid-thirties, living in his hometown of Rzeszów. He worked in IT as a software expert, an SAP and AutoCAD developer in the local Pratt & Whitney aircraft engine assembly plant. He'd helped organize the city's first Equality March event and was texting his friends—Kamil, in Kraków, and Paweł, also in Rzeszów—about what was happening.

The three had known each other for a few years through the center-left political party Razem, but none were professional politicians or activists. Like Kuba, Kamil had an ordinary job, working for a company outsourced to handle FedEx's finance operations. He came from the village of Łukowa in the conservative Nowa Sarzyna region.

"I wanted to be a doctor or a vet but didn't quite get the grades, so I studied biophysics. I lasted about a year and a half doing that," Kamil said. "It was pretty rough."

After Kamil left the university in Kraków in 2015, he moved to Birmingham, England's second-biggest city, where he worked for a couple of years.

"It opened my eyes a bit," Kamil said. "It's not like it was paradise, but after my very conservative hometown and conservative Kraków, I saw how things could be. One of my gay friends could walk along the street holding hands with her girlfriend, and no one would take any notice."

By 2017, Kamil was starting to think he should return home, partly because he missed his family and friends and also to see how he could advance LGBTQ+ rights in Poland.

"I was trying to join local organizations to see how I could help," Kamil said, "but I'm not sure why that did not work out. I emailed several requests and never received any reply. I was knocking on various doors here in Kraków, hoping to help, but there was no response."

Kamil began independently organizing small fundraising events in Kraków for Pride events elsewhere.

"I asked some friends to come," he recalled. "There was a DJ, a secondhand-book sale, that sort of thing. It wasn't a lot of money, but it helped."

In 2018, the organizers of the first-ever Equality March in Rzeszów, deep in Poland's highly conservative Podkarpackie region, invited Kamil to speak at the event.

"It was about thirty miles from my hometown, and I said yes. It was my first public speech," Kamil said.

His legs shook as he began to talk, looking out at about one hundred counterprotesters hurling abuse and threats at him. Kamil still keeps the text of that speech on his phone, and he read excerpts from it to me when we met in a Kraków café:

> I've spent most of my life in a small village nearby. I grew up in a conservative, homophobic family and attended a strict Catholic school. I was taught that loving a person of the same sex is a sin, something ugly. That's why I was never brave enough to say who I am, but today is the day when I'm saying loudly that I am gay, when I'm saying that I'm proud. I will not believe that the nature of my love is worse than anyone else's or that I'm a worse human being. I know that almost all of us are feeling fear, but we need to find the courage to act.

Until that very moment, Kamil had come out only to a close circle of friends—not to his family and certainly not to a crowd of over a thousand people. News of his speech soon reached his family and friends in Łukowa.

"I'd never come out to my parents. It was a shocker for them. Even my aunts were angry, as if what I said about the difficulties in my upbringing somehow reflected badly on the entire family," he said. "I don't think I'd do it the same way if I did it now." If he could do it differently, he'd come out directly to his parents, "so they wouldn't have to learn of it watching television."

While the reaction from Kamil's family was not good, far worse came from strangers, some of it horribly hostile.

"About fifteen people sent me terrible messages, including death threats. Only one person said anything supportive to me on Facebook. I remember crying over messages from people I'd gone to school with. One girl from my class sent me an invitation to be friends on Facebook, but I didn't respond because I didn't know if it was genuine or a trap."

After his speech, Kamil's parents and brother announced they were coming from their village to see him in Kraków.

"When they arrived, we just couldn't figure out how to talk about it as a family, so instead we sat around playing cards," he said. "But I knew my dad was really angry from the very aggressive way he was playing UNO."

The family tension took some time to fade, and going to visit them in his hometown meant Kamil risked abuse from the locals. He often asked friends to go with him on those trips.

"For a bit of support and protection," Kamil explained. "Sometimes I wore earphones, too, so I couldn't hear comments aimed at me on the street."

After running as a candidate in the 2018 local Kraków elections with a few others to raise awareness about LGBTQ+ issues—and losing—Kamil gave up activism. The election campaign had drained him. Feeling burnt out, he stepped back to rest. Then six months later, in 2019, his friend Kuba first messaged Kamil that his hometown was one of the municipalities preparing to pass an anti-LGBTQ+ resolution.

"I couldn't forget what it was like to be a teenager growing up there, with no one to talk to about being gay. How hard that was," said Kamil. "And I couldn't stop thinking about the young people there now, hearing from their local government that they're not welcome. I decided I had to do something."

Kuba started collecting data on which localities' councils were passing the resolutions. Soon after, he set up a WhatsApp group to discuss his findings with Kamil, Paweł, and another friend named Paulina. Paulina was an academic in Kielce, a city about one hundred miles northwest of Rzeszów, where Kuba and Paweł were based at the time.

Paulina told me, "The mainstream media in Poland weren't covering the issue closely, so I began to use my skills as a researcher by listing local authorities that adopted those resolutions, to show the massive scale of the homophobic campaign. First, I worked on my own, and then with Kuba, who invited me to collaborate on the project after he had published a list of the councils on Queer.pl [a website supporting the LGBTQ+ community] and I'd published my research on the Love Does Not Exclude/Miłość Nie Wyklucza website. Soon after, I met Kamil and Paweł."

The group started posting their findings online. Kuba said he expected some press interest, but he never imagined they were on the brink of a protracted legal battle. Meanwhile, Kamil sent a petition to his local council opposing the resolution.

"I wasn't brave enough to go there and to tell them that they were stupid and shouldn't do it," said Kamil. "I heard they were also collecting signatures for a petition to support the resolution. My mum told me that people coming out of Sunday Mass were signing the petition, but that she didn't."

Kamil needed to do something and felt they should push harder. Without really knowing where to start, he began "googling every politician in Europe I could think of so I could email them," he said, laughing. "It's not really the professional way to do it, but there I was, not knowing how else to do it, lying on my sofa with my laptop on my chest, emailing random politicians all over Europe."

Astonishingly, it worked.

"Someone from a Swedish political party invited Kuba and me to a meeting at the European Parliament in Strasbourg," Kamil recalled.

The two flew to the French city, where a debate was underway on LGBTQ+ rights, and spoke at a press conference after the meeting. With so much going on during the trip, they ended up missing their flight home.

"All this was new for me," remembered Kamil. "So we had to take a bus overnight from Frankfurt," he recalled.

When they got off the bus in Poland eighteen hours later, gritty and tired, they were shocked by the newspaper headlines that greeted them in the shops.

"We were on the front pages. Surreal," Kamil said. "The headlines called us traitors, said that we had ratted on Poland to Europe, that these issues should be dealt with internally, within the country, and that we shouldn't go complaining internationally. It was amazing. We had ratted on the country."

Kamil hadn't slept all night. When he arrived at work, his supervisor took one look at him and said, "Go home." When he told her he didn't have any more vacation days, she simply smiled and repeated: "Go home."

Having even a somewhat sympathetic workplace helped a lot.

"One advantage of working in a big international corporation is that no one cares much about you or what you're doing," Kamil said. "And my supervisor supported me. When foreign journalists would call to interview me, she gave me time to talk to them."

After the Strasbourg meeting, the campaign really took off.

Kamil recalled, “We didn’t have much experience, and sometimes human rights ‘professionals’ criticized us because we were trying everything.”

“Everything” included contacting foreign cities twinned with Polish municipalities—formal sister-city partnerships intended to promote cultural ties—in the hope of raising awareness.

“The professionals didn’t all approve, but we did it anyway,” Kamil said.

Paweł’s technical skills turned the data in Kuba’s spreadsheets into an online interactive map, which quickly became known as the Atlas of Hate. It transformed the campaign, laying out exactly which councils had passed the resolutions. People in Poland, Europe, and all over the world were looking closely at the map.

In those early days, the activists had no expectation of success.

“We simply wanted to protest the adoption of the resolutions,” recalled Kuba.

But as interest grew, the inexperienced activists looked for ways to push the campaign forward.

“We were trying to do everything,” said Kamil. “Sometimes we were invited to local debates. I remember going to one that was terrible. It was in a town hall, and the atmosphere was terribly hostile. Some guy thought it was funny to dress up as a woman, all in pink with balloons pushed down his shirt. And I was up against experienced politicians. I didn’t do very well. One of the women debating me was just full of hatred.”

Even years later, Kamil winced at the memory.

“I could see it in her eyes,” he said. “She wasn’t against us for political reasons or to pursue her own advancement; she really meant it. The virulent hatred running through her really shook me. I’d never seen that up close before. She was saying we had betrayed Poland, that we were traitors. Afterwards, I left the hall in tears.”

Despite setbacks like that one, as news of the campaign spread across Europe, the amateur activists suddenly found themselves in demand. Initially, they lacked the funds for travel.

"We were invited to a lot of places, like the Pride events in Copenhagen," said Kamil. "Even though the organizers covered expenses, we had to pay for them up front and then ask to be reimbursed. Thankfully, some of my friends were able to lend us the money." What was galling, he said, was "at some of these events you'd hear these professional activists, paid to be there, complaining that the hotel had been nicer the previous year."

Their success in generating attention for the Atlas and the punitive resolutions quickly triggered a fierce backlash. Starting in 2020, seven local governments sued the activists behind the Atlas of Hate. Kuba recounted how each of the lawsuits demanded the same thing—that the group "pay twenty thousand *zloty* [around $5,000] to a local conservative organization, [and] apologize in front of the European Parliament in Brussels and at a press conference at the Polish Press Agency." Kuba estimated that the total cost, including the apology trip to Brussels, would have been more than $50,000. Letters informing the activists they were being sued were even sent to their workplaces, obliging them to disclose the cases to their bosses.

Because the group was composed of four friends and not part of a formally registered organization, their legal status was confusing to the parties suing them.

"We were just a group of individuals," recalled Kamil, "so sometimes they sued some of us but not all of us. And they weren't very competent. There's a carpenter in my hometown with the same name as mine, and they sent the court documents to him by mistake."

Fighting the lawsuits was exhausting.

"It was a long, drawn-out process with letters being exchanged by their lawyers and our lawyers for months," Kamil said.

Kuba is hard of hearing and relies on lipreading, so when we met in Rzeszów for dinner, we sat next to each other and typed out our conversation on our phones. He told me he felt particularly targeted as a person with hearing issues.

"I don't understand speech by ear," he said, "and so I needed a written hearing, via chat during a remote hearing, or by traditional paper correspondence."

Nevertheless, the Ordo Iuris lawyer always demanded Kuba's personal presence in court, even though it was neither necessary nor something that was required of the other defendants. "They tried to make the process as burdensome as possible for me," he said.

The hearings were conducted online, taking around twelve to fourteen days in all. The activists had to use up their vacation time from their jobs for the court sessions. Kamil remembers that despite reassurances from their lawyers that their chances of winning were good, the court cases were extremely stressful and involved juggling their work responsibilities at the same time.

"Even if we were 90 percent sure of winning, it's always there in the back of your mind that the courts could rule against you. . . . Once I was working at home in my parents' house and I had an online court case that same day," said Kamil. "I finished doing something for work and jumped to the next room, where I had to be on camera because a judge was asking me a question. And I realized that my hair was all over the place like I just woke up."

The court processes dragged out over years.

The legal team for the group was headed by the legendary human rights lawyer Karolina Gierdal, who had defended LGBTQ+ rights cases in Poland and at the European Court of Human Rights. And there was an outpouring of support from every quarter, including allies in the media, such as prominent photographer Bart Staszewski, whose pictures supporting the campaign went viral.

Kuba explained: "There was a lot of grassroots activity—letters, articles, requests for public information, petitions, court speeches, notifications to the prosecutor's office, participation in consultations, lobbying in EU institutions, speeches at assemblies and conferences, street demonstrations, and so on."

Support also came from national and international NGOs and politicians, as well as some sympathetic local councilors. Inside the government, discreet allies forwarded them useful documents, sometimes anonymously, revealing what was happening in local authority offices.

What had started out as a concrete wall of opposition began to crack unexpectedly. Faced with mounting consequences, including court defeats that often meant paying costs of up to twenty-one thousand *zloty* ($5,000), the councils began to reverse their resolutions, sometimes very suddenly. By April 2025, the last of these resolutions had been scrapped, ending a dark chapter in the country's local politics. Against all the odds, the group of four inexperienced activists had taken on powerful government forces and won.

Part of what worked was the threat of funding cuts or the actual withdrawal of funds from councils that passed the resolutions. According to Kuba, Świdnica, a town that was the second local authority to pass the resolution, in March 2019, lost forty million *zloty* (around $10 million) in grant monies from the European Economic Area (EEA). This grant, provided by the governments of Iceland, Liechtenstein, and Norway to tackle economic inequality in Europe, had been earmarked for building a municipal meeting center and renovating the marketplace. Kuba also estimated that Świdnica lost four million *zloty* ($1 million) more from the EU that had been intended to support programs for unemployed people.

Other councils, including those of Podkarpackie, Radzyń Podlaski, and Wilamowice, were each denied around seven million *zloty* ($2 million) that they had hoped to use for cultural and other local projects. The European Commission President Ursula von der Leyen said, "LGBTQI-free zones are humanity-free zones."

The campaign to alert towns and cities across Europe, twinned with the various councils—a tactic Kamil said professional NGO staff had warned them against—proved highly significant. The move was a variation of the ostracization tactic developed in 1880s Ireland as part of the boycott campaign outlined in the Introduction to this book. For example, the Irish city of Fermoy ended its cooperation with Nowa Dęba, and the French city of Saint-Jean-de-Braye ended its partnership with Tuchów. The Polish city of Puławy lost partnerships with Nieuwegein in the Netherlands and Douai in France. France's Loire Valley region terminated its partnership with the Małopolska Provinces, the Belgian city of Puurs broke off with Dębica, and the Italian village of Alpette pulled out of a planned partnership with Poniatowa.

In early 2021, Kamil emailed his hometown council, asking them to revoke their resolution.

"I was just going through the motions, saying why it was a bad idea and so on," Kamil recalled with some incredulity. "I cc'd a friend on it. When the local authority responded, I didn't bother opening it because I knew it would just be the usual nonsense."

As he was about to press "Delete" on the email reply, another email popped up, from the friend he had included in the message, saying the council was going to cancel the resolution.

"I couldn't believe it," said Kamil, "so I read the email from the council and saw that, yes, they had decided to revoke it."

Many of the councils tried to quietly and quickly drop the resolutions.

"Often without discussion, in silence and in shame," Kuba said. "The Świdnica district only published the agenda of their meeting hours before they voted to repeal the resolution, and in other places, the full titles of the repealed resolutions weren't given—only their corresponding numbers—while information on how councilors voted could only be obtained by submitting official public information requests."

The activists' stunning victories resonated far beyond Poland. The group was nominated for the prestigious Sakharov Prize, awarded by the European Parliament (which ultimately went to Belarus's democratic opposition), and they won a host of national and international awards.

Paulina, the academic who also worked on the campaign, highlighted the enormous effort behind it. The resolutions were "an extreme manifestation of systemic discrimination against LGBTQ+ people—a lack of marriage equality, adequate transition procedures, or protection for rainbow families, queer teenagers, and non-heteronormative seniors, who are particularly vulnerable to violence," she said. "In recent years, I spent so much time on court proceedings, which we managed to win despite political pressure and systemic homophobia. I am now trying to reclaim that time for both my family and my research."

The others agreed that the victories came at considerable personal cost.

Kamil said, "We spent hundreds of hours on behalf of the Atlas of Hate, appealing to local authorities, monitoring local governments, contacting politicians and international institutions. For LGBT people, these were years of proving that we deserve dignity and respect, that our love is not inferior, that we are not inferior."

I asked them whether, despite their spectacular victories, there was anything they would have done differently.

Kuba laughed and said, "In one of my court statements, I ventured into an exposition of sociological considerations about fascism. The court didn't really refer to this in its judgment, so I think it would have been better to stick to arguments about legal precedents."

Kamil said that he would "take care of myself better, of my health. It's not only about you, but about how you are with other people. I remember—and I'm not proud of it—that sometimes when I was tired, I wasn't always the nicest guy. Not because I'm not a good person, but because I was exhausted."

Taylor Swift's album *The Life of a Showgirl* started blaring from the ceiling speakers in the new coffee shop where we were meeting, and Kamil interrupted his thoughts to complain about it.

"She's better than this," he said. "The lyrics on these new tracks aren't up to her usual standard."

Then, going right back to lessons learned from the campaign, he continued: "I wasn't taking care of myself at all. I was eating badly, sleeping badly, and all my free time was spent on this campaign. It was totally chaotic. If I'd rested, maybe I would have been able to plan things better and be more efficient."

A lot has changed for Kamil since the end of the campaign.

"I've lost around sixty kilos [130 pounds], I quit smoking, and I started running, cycling, and swimming. I feel stronger now—I feel great," he said.

Kamil has now finished his studies in accounting and is taking a break from activism. And things are a lot better now with his family.

"A year ago, there was a Polish TV series with storylines about gay relationships," he said. "Honestly, it wasn't great TV, but my parents asked, 'Can we watch this together?' I really appreciated that. It had all been a shock for them, and they needed time to process it."

His brother now posts supportive messages about him on social media.

Paweł reflected on how the campaign took on a life of its own, with greater impact than they had ever imagined.

"When we started, we didn't think about winning," he said. "We were four activists trying to take on over a hundred local governments. We were driven more by the need to express our opposition than by any expectation of success. The most important lesson we can take away from the history of the Atlas of Hate today is the awareness that sometimes even inconspicuous actions, such as a sheet of paper with a list of resolutions and a simple map, can contribute to real change."

CHAPTER 10

HAJRIJA ČOBO, BOSNIA

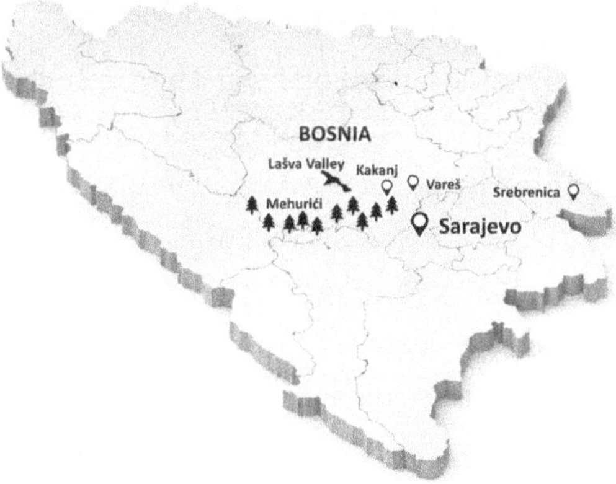

"I was a strange kid," Hajrija Čobo said, laughing.

She was talking as she drove me from the central Bosnian town of Kakanj to the ancient forest of Mehurići, an area she has spent years trying to protect from an international mining enterprise.

"I was always reading, learning about herbs and cooking. I was a little bit introverted," Hajrija said, a claim that defies belief when you spend time with her. "I found other children boring. When the girls were playing with dolls, I was making creams from herbs to treat cuts and wounds. I started baking cakes and preparing meals when I was five years old. My parents were so patient. I mean, you can't imagine the mess. I ruined the kitchen more than once."

It was late November 2025 when we met for the first time. As we drove up the mountain, the dense woods flashing by on the roadside were covered in snow.

"There are wolves in here, bears, foxes, mountain cats, and so many other wild animals," Hajrija said. "Fish, freshwater crabs, too, and all sorts of birds. There are trees here that probably remember my great-great-grandfather as a boy playing among them. Three hundred fifty to four hundred years old. The roots of those trees are bigger than I am. It's amazing, isn't it? We have great pride in this forest. And we must protect it at all costs."

Hajrija grew up in Kakanj during the 1980s and 1990s with her parents and older brother. Kakanj is considered Europe's oldest continuously inhabited settlement, dating back to the Neolithic Age, as early as 6800 B.C.E. Today it has a population of about thirty-six thousand. For more than a century, Kakanj has been a coal-mining town and a busy industrial hub. It is home to a massive coal-fired power plant that generates a significant share of the country's electricity and is one of the region's largest emitters of sulfur dioxide, a harmful gas linked to respiratory illness. The town also has a large cement factory.

While these industries have long been the backbone of the local economy, they have taken a heavy toll on the environment. Industrial pollution is a major national issue. Bosnia produces two-thirds of its electricity from coal, burning through approximately thirteen million metric tons a year. According to a 2019 World Bank report, 3,300 people die prematurely each year in Bosnia due to exposure to air pollution, constituting nearly 10 percent of all deaths. The Bosnian capital of Sarajevo is ranked as one of the world's most polluted cities by Swiss company IQAir, which operates an air-quality data platform.

Hajrija said her father, a painter and decorator, taught her to read and write in the evening when she was very young.

"The next day I'd have done the task he set," she recalled, "like writing the letters *Aa* in capitals and small letters on a page, then *Bb,* and so on."

Thanks to her father, Hajrija could read and write at age four, so she was a precocious student when she entered school. She said when the teachers got to know her, they would test her only at the end of the course rather than lesson by lesson, knowing her voracious reading would mean she had absorbed all the study materials.

As she grew older, Hajrija was never drawn to the bright lights of the big city of Sarajevo, thirty miles south of Kakanj.

"I may have been a challenge, but I never snuck out for joy rides at night," she said.

Her main escape from the rigors of school and the hometown air pollution was the Mehurići forest, a thirty-minute drive into the mountains from her childhood home.

"We would go there every weekend," she recalled. "My uncle was a forester and had a cottage deep in the woods. There was a small community there, and in the basement of his cottage was a bakery."

The cottage was a child's paradise: Geese, horses, and ducks roamed freely on the property. The smell of baking bread seeped up through the floorboards.

"I've felt a connection to that place for as long as I can remember," Hajrija said.

Her bond with nature is profound. She said riding horses came easily to her from the first time she tried: "It feels just like flying, so fulfilling."

As we drove farther up the mountain road, she kept naming increasingly obscure species found in these woods. She also recalled, in vivid detail, the times she was bitten by snakes and had pictures of the bites to prove it.

Life for Hajrija became much tougher during her teenage years, as Bosnia, then a republic within Yugoslavia, was descending into a bitter civil war. Yugoslavia had united six republics and many ethnic groups, including Bosniaks, Serbs, Croats, Slovenes, and Albanians, under President Tito's iron-fisted policy "Brotherhood and Unity." But after Tito's death in 1980, the delicate balance that held Yugoslavia together began to collapse. Economic troubles and rising nationalism pushed republics toward independence. Slovenia and Croatia broke away in 1991, provoking a violent response from the Serb-led Yugoslav army. Thousands were killed before UN-brokered ceasefires paused fighting in 1992. Bosnia, the most ethnically mixed republic—made up of predominantly Muslim Bosniaks, Christian Serbs, and Catholic Croats—tried to become independent next. Bosnian Serb leaders, backed by Serbia, resisted and launched a brutal campaign of ethnic cleansing that displaced at least two million people and killed about one hundred thousand—approximately 80 percent of whom were Bosniaks.

Sarajevo was besieged for nearly four years as UN peacekeepers often proved powerless, and international diplomacy failed to stop the fighting.

"Those days were hard," Hajrija said.

Her dad joined the police force but received no salary, and her brother, a teenager at the time, got a job in a bakery. Her family had a cottage outside Kakanj with a small garden where her mother grew vegetables—enough, Hajrija said, "to feed half of our apartment block."

Hajrija sold cigarettes and coffee beans on the street, and people sometimes paid her in gold.

"They'd give me a small gold ring for five cigarettes," recalled Hajrija. "That's when I learned that gold has no value in a catastrophe. Because people don't really need gold, right? If you can't eat it, it has no value. What's precious in bad times? It's land where you can grow food, coffee, or even tobacco."

Despite the mayhem and violence raging all around them, Kakanj was "a strange island of peace" and a sanctuary for people from nearby villages that were under attack.

"The war didn't hit us as directly as many other places," Hajrija said.

Thirty miles to the northwest of the town, at Lašva Valley, between 1992 and 1994, the military Croatian Defense Council (HVO) carried out mass murder, rape, and imprisonment against local Bosniaks. One hundred miles east of Kakanj, Bosnian Serb forces and paramilitaries killed more than eight thousand Bosniak men and boys in the mountain town of Srebrenica in July 1995. The town had previously been declared a UN "safe area," under its protection. The massacre was the first legally recognized genocide in Europe since the end of the Second World War.

The fighting around Kakanj often meant it was impossible to get food and other supplies into the town from outside. Hajrija's family and neighbors relied on each other heavily during those years.

"People from all over Yugoslavia were in our apartment building—we're a family of Bosnian Muslims, but there were Croatians, Montenegrins, Slovenians, Serbians. We shared food; we shared whatever we had. We stuck together and got on with it," said Hajrija.

The shortages also included textbooks at school.

"That just made me do more research in the library," Hajrija recalled. "I would look at a whole shelf of books at the library and read them all, left to right in order, one by one. You can never have too much knowledge, right?"

During the war, her home often had no electricity, so Hajrija read by streetlight, which was still working most of the time.

The war ended in 1995 after NATO air strikes and gains by Bosniak and Croat forces pushed the Bosnian Serbs to the negotiating table. The US-brokered Dayton Accords split Bosnia into two entities, a Bosnian Serb republic and a Muslim-Croat federation, loosely bound by a central government. By then, Yugoslavia was unraveling: Slovenia, Croatia, Bosnia, and Macedonia were independent, and Montenegro would follow later.

After the war, Hajrija became an English teacher. Recalling a conversation with a fellow student at college in late 1999 who said Hajrija would never get the qualifications necessary for the job, she laughed.

"Yeah, I did it out of spite," Hajrija said. "I was offended when that woman said I wouldn't be able to do it, you know. So I did it to prove I could."

Today, she loves her job teaching sixteen- to eighteen-year-olds at two high schools in Kakanj.

"I'm teaching them how to argue back, how to think for themselves," she said.

Hajrija's English is impeccable, unusual for someone who's never lived in an English-speaking country. Though she learned some of the language from Hollywood movies and rock music, she carries no trace of an American accent or vocabulary. She has an authentic English accent and uses words like "autumn" and "half past one."

We continued up the mountain she visited often as a child. Despite the freezing temperatures outside, she passed me an iced latte in a takeout cup from the stock on her back seat.

"Drink, drink," she urged. "It's the Bosnian way. Coffee all the time."

I dutifully gulped it back. "How many coffees do you have a day?" I asked. "Four?"

"Four? Four?" she whooped. "Maybe four at breakfast, yes."

But Hajrija's hyper energy is based on more than caffeine. She gives off such a natural, powerful electric force you wonder if her phone charges just from being in her pocket. Her obsessive drive for learning led her to start studying for a law degree in 2017, and she has since completed two master's degrees in law. She is in the process of qualifying to practice as a lawyer.

On Wednesday, May 25, 2022, the day after her last master's exam, she wanted to go to the forest for some peace and quiet.

"I needed a day off," she said. "My mother and I took my dogs and drove to our favorite spot on the mountain. When we got there, instead of the restorative silence of the forest, we found excavators, industrial machines, and men in hard hats working. It was all a terrible noise. I was totally shocked. I couldn't speak. I thought, 'It's like someone stole our place. They're ruining everything.'"

Recovering her senses, Hajrija started taking pictures of the machines with her phone.

"I was so angry, I didn't care who was behind this, I was going to fight them," she said, taking her hands off the steering wheel and throwing shadow punches in the air. "I thought, 'This is my place from childhood; my aunt and uncle used to live there. That's my silent place, my place for solitude, and I want it back. So, no, you can't take it.'"

What Hajrija saw that day was the ground clearing for a cement plant—the first visible stage of a new mining operation by UK-based company Adriatic Metals. The roughly $200 million project aims to extract mostly silver, zinc, and lead, as well as smaller amounts of gold and copper, from the border between two municipalities, Vareš and Kakanj. These metals were intended to be shipped to smelters around Europe, including Belgium, Germany, Italy, and Spain. Analysts say these metals are crucial to the EU's efforts to reduce its dependence on Chinese and Russian raw materials. But Hajrija said very little information about the project was shared with the public, and in the spring of 2022, it was still a mystery to most of the locals.

Hajrija went home, spent a few days pondering what to do, and then sat down and wrote a long post on Facebook that she shared on multiple accounts.

"I pretended it was from a group of people," said Hajrija, "although in truth it was only me."

The tactic was effective. Soon enough, others joined Hajrija, supporting her complaints on social media. Most stayed anonymous, but an informal group of about twenty people formed under the name Park prirode Trstionica i Boriva (Trstionica and Boriva Nature Park) and launched a campaign called Zaštitimo Mehurići–Kakanj (Let's Protect Mehurići–Kakanj) to oppose the arrival of harmful industry there. The activists soon discovered that someone from the local council assembly had been asking questions about the Adriatic Metals venture six months earlier, but information about what had happened next was hard to find.

Hajrija wrote to the local and regional governments, demanding answers about the project and whether it was legal. She said the official answer from the local municipality was that they didn't know what was going on.

"It was unbelievable. I wanted that concrete plant moved out of there. So we took them on," she said.

The activists decided to use the local government's byzantine bureaucracy against itself. One Monday morning in early June, just a week or so after she had come across the cement plant in the forest, Hajrija and the other activists flooded municipality offices with emails requesting information about the project. They worded the requests so that the local officials would have to download all their emails and attached photos and then pass all those messages individually on to colleagues at the canton (district) level. The activists made the same requests via the official contacts on the messaging app Viber. The tactic completely jammed the local government system.

"They had to spend all day downloading the attachments in the emails and recording them separately, even though they contained identical information. They had to respond to all the emails. It paralyzed their systems." Hajrija laughed.

It soon came to light that the mining company had never obtained the necessary permissions or fulfilled the compliance measures needed to start work in the area. The reaction was swift. Within a week, the owner of the cement plant, who was subcontracted by Adriatic Metals, asked for a meeting with Hajrija. She went to the site of the project on the mountainside to see him, in no mood to negotiate.

"I just want your industry out of here, off this site," she told him.

The cement company backed down and almost immediately started to move everything away. But the Adriatic Metals mining operation was still going forward, farther up the mountain.

Hajrija stopped the car on the muddy mountain track to show me where the site had been. "Over there were trucks and various earth moving machines," she said, pointing. "And over there, containers and stone crushers."

Though the site was blanketed in snow, telltale mounds of disturbed earth were still visible.

"I promised the birds here I would bring their homes back," Hajrija said. "They were driven out for a year by the constant noise of the concrete plant, day and night. There was no birdsong at all."

After another short drive, we stopped to eat lunch at a nearby restaurant on the mountain. Hajrija ordered trout for both of us. Despite the freezing weather, we went outside so she could smoke while we waited for the fish to be served. Standing next to a table used for picnics in the summer, she told me more about the research that she and her fellow activists did after discovering the mining project.

"We found out it was not only a danger to biodiversity, but also a very direct threat to the health of the local population," she said.

Kakanj's water supply comes from a river that is fed by streams from the Vareš area. According to Hajrija, the water supply has already been contaminated with heavy metals and has not been drinkable since the spring of 2022.

"We know this because we've been conducting our own small-scale water tests and reaching out to local experts and leading professors," Hajrija explained.

Research on how mining has affected the health of the local population is extremely limited. But a December 2025 news report revealed that all forty-four residents of Vareš who had their blood tested for lead—at the request of a Canadian investor—showed contamination, with seventeen requiring urgent medical attention. The residents tested were living near the mine site.

Director of the Vareš Health Center Ahmed Memić told the newspaper that the wider population should have their blood tested, not just people living close to the mine. "We have notified all competent institutions and ministries at the federal and cantonal levels and requested urgent measures to manage this situation. We can't respond to this alone on a local level," he said. Nevertheless, the newspaper report concluded, "[of] additional concern is the silence of the authorities in the Zenica-Doboj canton and the Federation of Bosnia and Herzegovina, who have still not made any public statement fourteen days after receiving these results."

Hajrija finally finished her cigarette.

"Aren't you cold?" I asked, shivering and hinting that it was time to go back inside.

"Not really." She shrugged and lit another cigarette.

Apparently oblivious to the piercingly cold temperature, Hajrija finished her second cigarette, then scooped snow from the tabletop and rubbed it between her fingers to clean her hands. When we returned inside, people in the restaurant waved and said they recognized her from Facebook.

In October 2022, Hajrija reported the mining venture and the growing local concerns about environmental damage to the Bern Convention, part of an international treaty that protects wildlife and natural habitats in Europe and in some African countries as well. If there's a concern that a government is violating the treaty, complaints can be made to the Convention's Standing Committee, based at the Council of Europe in Strasbourg, France. If the committee opens a case, the relevant government has to explain itself publicly and report back. That kind of scrutiny can be very damaging for companies, and reputational fallout is often one of the committee's most effective forms of influence.

Hajrija's complaint to the Standing Committee noted that the concession for exploration and exploitation of minerals in Vareš and surrounding areas was granted despite very limited information about its environmental impact and a lack of public participation in any review process. She told the committee that the area is "rich in biodiversity, with habitats for numerous unique algae, surrounding flora, fish, and crabs. There is also an important migratory bird route overhead." She went on to argue that the mining activities and deforestation would critically endanger the ecosystem. Hajrija also noted that Kakanj's water supply comes from the Bukovica River, which is fed by streams from Vareš. In her submission, she told the committee that the riverbed had already been affected by the mine runoff and that heavy metals would further impact the water, soil, and air.

Adriatic Metals has repeatedly rejected all of Hajrija's claims, trying to portray itself as a force for good by bringing foreign business acumen to Bosnia. If it weren't for the mine opening, Vareš would have remained nothing more than "the place at the end of the train line," said Adriatic Metals board member Sanela Karic during the facility's opening ceremony. The company has emphasized that it has employed more than two hundred people for the mining project and said it is contributing 2 percent of Bosnia's GDP. The Bosnian government has fully supported the company's activities in Vareš, declaring it a "project of special importance."

Undaunted, Hajrija had counterarguments at the ready. "While these hills around Vareš have always held the key to our industrial prosperity," she asserted, "the native-born competence that we once had has diminished as the best professional people began to leave our country. My government is endangering the lives of about forty thousand people in my town. For the sake of profit for a British company and jobs for a couple of hundred people. Do you know what that's called? It's called neocolonialism."

The Bern Convention committee met in September 2023 to consider Hajrija's case, declaring that it was "preoccupied with some of the concerns raised." It formally requested that both parties (most notably the authorities) "provide reports containing relevant updates on these matters for the next Bureau meeting in Spring 2024." Crucially, the committee "called for the authorities to enforce a halt to any ongoing exploitation until the facts have been made clear."

But the mining never stopped, and some of the environmental damage caused by the company is irreparable. "The works are carried out on a hill with a water system that permeates the subsoil just as the body is permeated with veins," explained Hajrija. "Once you release heavy metals into the groundwater, it's over; there's no going back."

Three months after the Bern Convention ordered the suspension of the project, Adriatic Metals sued Hajrija for defamation, saying she had spread false information about the firm in interviews and on social media. It was a classic Strategic Lawsuit against Public Participation (SLAPP) suit—a civil case about alleged defamation that can lead to demands for huge compensation, frequently used against activists across Europe.

"The court sent me the legal papers in a big pink envelope, like a giant birthday card." Hajrija laughed. "It arrived on December 10 [International Human Rights Day]. I knew what it was and didn't bother opening it. It was the end of the semester, and I needed to focus on my students' exams. My mother lives with me, and she asked me what was in the envelope. I told her it was a lawsuit. She started crying and asked, 'Will you go to jail?'"

Hajrija was much less troubled by it than her mother. The documents lay unopened for two weeks. She finished her students' exams and left for the forest to think about what to do.

Hajrija had thirty days to respond to the lawsuit. She finally read the charges against her, which stated that in her media interviews and on Facebook, she had defamed the company. As she looked things over, Hajrija concluded that if she got a lawyer, it would be a slow and painful process to show how best to defend her. She would have to explain all the information and data, and tell the lawyer how to connect all the dots.

"So I thought I might as well do it myself," Hajrija explained.

At 10:00 p.m. the night before the mid-January deadline, she sat down at her computer for twenty-two hours straight and wrote her response to the lawsuit. Fueled by countless coffees, she chain-smoked through the night and the next day, banging out a 473-page defense.

"Honestly, I had a great time," Hajrija said. "I work best under pressure; I love it. Adriatic Metals had uploaded some documents on its website that it probably didn't mean to, about water analysis and permits, so I used all that, quoting their own data against them."

Hajrija sent off the document with two CDs of evidence, including pictures of what the mining operations were doing to the forest, only just making the deadline.

In April 2024, the company abruptly withdrew the lawsuit.

She continued the story as we made our way back down the mountain. "It was such a humiliation for them. I guess they thought I'd be too intimidated to respond, then, 'Bam!'—473 pages back at them." Hajrija cackled, smacking the steering wheel with her palm.

Although the withdrawal was a real victory, it also meant Hajrija wouldn't get the chance to cross-examine the company's executives about their accusations. She initially refused to consent to the case's being dropped, hoping this would force the court to bring the matter before a judge.

"I thought that would be fun—an epic court hearing." She laughed.

Nevertheless, in late June, the court issued its own verdict without a trial, siding with Hajrija and officially closing the case. It was a triumph for Hajrija. "This was much better than the company just withdrawing its lawsuit," she said. "The ruling proved the company was wrong."

The outcome in the case has inspired other environmental activists by showing them they can stand up to large corporations that try to set the rules.

"They thought someone without any previous experience wouldn't dare take on this huge company. Well . . . hold my glass, let me dry my nails, and I will show you how you win against a big corporation. They were beaten by someone they thought was just some crazy cat lady," she said, laughing.

For the record, Hajrija has seven cats and two dogs.

"They were strays with nowhere to go. What could I do?" she said, shrugging.

After the verdict, Hajrija began to attract international support. The international NGO Front Line Defenders publicized her case, and in June 2024, United Nations Special Rapporteur for Human Rights Defenders Mary Lawlor visited Hajrija to learn more about her work.

International solidarity helped Hajrija a lot.

"It's just like the animal world," she said. "Those who are weak and alone will be eaten. If you have others to support you and back you, you will be safe. The lawsuit was such a huge mistake for them. It meant people all over the world knew for the first time what Adriatic Metals was doing here on our land. Shit, when they sued me, it brought so much more attention to what they were up to."

We stopped for a moment to get some fresh water from a pipe sticking out between some rocks on the mountainside.

"I always take the water from this spring," she said, filling her bottle. "It's so clean—you can keep it for a month, and it doesn't get stale."

Hajrija explained more about the legal battles over the mining project that followed, noting that the fight has taken various twists and turns. An October 2023 complaint about Adriatic Metals cutting down trees was rejected. In July 2024, the country's Constitutional Court overturned a national government decision that had granted the company temporary use of more than seventy-two thousand square meters of the state-owned forest in Vareš. However, the Constitutional Court ruling was never implemented. In December 2024, a regional court annulled the permit allowing Adriatic Metals to mine in the region, saying the authorities "should have clarified whether the proposed mineral extraction and construction of related facilities would negatively impact the Bukovica water source." But only fifteen days later, the national government issued a brand-new authorization. The mining has never stopped.

In September 2025, Adriatic Metals was bought by Canadian conglomerate Dundee Precious Metals, now called DPM Metals Inc.

"With the addition of the Vareš operation, DPM is a premier mining business with a peer-leading growth profile and a high-quality development and exploration pipeline," enthused the company's President and CEO David Rae. Rae promised that DPM would "optimize and realize Vareš's full value potential." His statement made no mention of the company's obligations or intentions to protect the environment or the forest's habitat.

Hajrija believes that the mining was approved and allowed to continue, despite all the court rulings and popular protests, because of the financial corruption that has long plagued Bosnia. She said she was even offered money to stop her activities. In Transparency International's 2025 Corruption Perceptions Index, Bosnia and Herzegovina rated 109th out of 182 countries listed and showed a steady decline in performance over the last decade.

Hajrija has also received dozens of death threats on Facebook since becoming an activist, not all anonymous. She took screenshots of them and passed them on to the police, who usually acted fast to contact the perpetrator.

"The police have been very supportive of me," she said. "I know that's not the case for most activists, but my father was in the police here, and they've all known me since I was a child, and they know what I'm trying to do here. They've been good."

As we moved on through towering trees and crossed trickling streams, Hajrija spoke of how Kakanj has changed over the years and of the lingering pain left by the war. The municipality's population dropped from its prewar 1991 level of fifty-six thousand to thirty-six thousand in 2013.

"Many of my friends left Kakanj during the war and never came back," she said. "And the most painful part of all this is that nobody talks about what happened . . . houses burnt, families forced to move, all the refugees. They're just silent about it all, and that still hurts today."

Still, according to Hajrija, the campaign to save the forest is uniting people who were enemies a generation ago. Veterans who fought for different armies in the '90s have now come together to protest the mining.

At the edge of the forest is Kraljeva Sutjeska, the famous fourteenth-century monastery. It has a collection of rare books, many of them printed before 1500. More than a century later, the Sultan Mehmed II Fatih Mosque, a national monument and one of the oldest preserved buildings from the Ottoman period, was built nearby, shortly after the 1463 conquest of Bosnia.

Hajrija and I walked along near the monastery and mosque and stopped to look at the display of four huge Advent candles outside the monastery in preparation for Christmas.

"These places of worship are a huge part of the heritage around here," she said. "I'm Muslim and don't celebrate Christmas in a religious way, but I love the holiday movies, being cozy, the whole atmosphere."

As we walked on, Hajrija spoke about the value of what matters and what doesn't.

"People who oppose me think of me as a witch. But this witch can't be bribed or bought." She laughed, shaking her head. "Why would I need two houses? I'm not interested in any offers of money to make me stop. I can't stand this obsession with gold. What really matters, especially in these dark days, is land where you can grow your own food. This will always have value."

The strange kid from Kakanj has become a formidable activist.

"I'm not normal." She laughed. "I'm very happy to be awkward. At least I know it and accept it. I don't always want to go along with what everyone else wants, and it's a great strength."

Hajrija is still actively campaigning to stop the mining operations on her beloved mountain.

CHAPTER 11

THE ELVES, THE BALTICS

For many years I'd heard whispers about the Baltic Elves, a mysterious group working clandestinely to counter online Russian propaganda. Created by volunteers in Lithuania in 2014, the Elves quickly achieved near-mythical status across Europe, their secrecy only enhancing their cachet.

Lithuania is one of the three Baltic states. To her north lies Latvia. Farther north still sits Estonia. All three are small countries, members of the former USSR. Lithuania, the largest of the three, is about the size of West Virginia, with a population of just under three million, about the same as Kansas. It sits on the northeastern edge of the European Union, and also borders Poland, the pro-Russian country of Belarus, and the freestanding Russian exclave Kaliningrad.

Locating and meeting a Baltic Elf isn't easy. Their strict privacy is their main protection. After months of searching, trying various contacts, and sending many emails, I found one of them, who agreed to meet me in the Lithuanian capital of Vilnius. I waited at a table next to the window in the coffee shop at the prearranged time, scanning passersby trudging through the rain for likely candidates. Then a tall, bearded man about my age suddenly appeared behind me, smiling and extending his hand.

"Giedrius Sakalauskas: Baltic Elf," he said.

Giedrius took a seat, ordered a coffee, and explained that although nearly all the elves remain anonymous, it was decided that he should be a spokesperson.

"There are two ways to maximize your safety," he said. "Either be totally private or, like me, totally public. Sometimes there are death threats on my Facebook page, but it's just part of leading this sort of life. I understand that."

It was Giedrius and two friends who started the movement, with no blueprint or model to copy from anywhere else.

"We three founding fathers of the elves started in a very simple way," he said. "Russia invaded Ukraine in 2014, and we saw all these lies in the comments sections below online news stories. Lies claiming NATO was useless, the EU was collapsing, Russia was saving Ukraine, and Lithuania was failing."

The three friends decided that doing something to counter these falsehoods was better than doing nothing.

"We went to the comments sections and posted information that was true," Giedrius told me. "It was as primitive as that, just to change what was being said. We needed to do something, and not just sit around and complain to each other about everything."

Neither Giedrius nor his friends had any specialist training in countering propaganda or fighting disinformation, and all three had ordinary jobs.

"I was working in the entertainment business, then in e-commerce," Giedrius said. "One of the other guys was doing similar types of jobs, and one was an academic lecturer."

Within days, others joined their efforts, countering the disinformation in their comments wherever they found it, and the Elves were underway.

"We were very successful very quickly, changing the proportion of disinformation in the news sections—from eighty to twenty against us to fifty-fifty and then to eighty to twenty in our favor," said Giedrius.

The volunteer network quickly and quietly gathered more and more recruits, with their activity then shifting to Facebook, where more discussions about news articles were taking place. Giedrius shared that the front line of disinformation is still on Facebook, saying that responding there is crucial because if disinformation goes unanswered, it multiplies exponentially.

"The beauty of the story is that nobody remembers who first came up with the elf name," said Giedrius, smiling and stroking his beard. "No one's claiming copyright. But the logic is pretty simple: We were fighting these online disinformation trolls. They're ugly and dark and full of hate. We're the opposite—bright and joyful and full of love, fighting those dark forces. The trolls are our enemy, so that makes us elves."

Much about the elves remains secret, but informed estimates put the current number of Baltic Elves at around five thousand. Working clandestinely was a founding principle and remains vital.

"We talked about ourselves as elves privately, but we were not public at all. Then, later in 2014, at a conference in the Latvian capital Riga, a man got up and gave a speech and said that the Baltic Elves exist. We thought it was a disaster. We felt betrayed. We wanted to stay anonymous and didn't want anything about our work to be known. We felt we had been put in danger. But then, somehow, the name took off; it became trendy to be an elf. Suddenly we were fashionable, we were cool." Giedrius laughed.

Nevertheless, secrecy is still paramount.

"Like Fight Club, the first rule of the Baltic Elves is that the elves don't exist," said Giedrius, grinning. "We decided early on to have a cell structure, where each small group is isolated from the rest within a larger honeycomb. We've never had big meetings or conferences. The less you know, the safer you are. We're not paranoid, but it's a simple way to keep yourself and your colleagues safe. We're fighting some very professional bad guys."

Russia uses disinformation warfare as a key part of its military strategy. It invests heavily in creating huge troll farms, where fake news is posted by a combination of real people and automation bots to flood social media with propaganda. Their main goals include undermining Western democracies, attacking the Ukrainian government, promoting fear and chaos, and making truth itself seem unknowable. For example, since Ukraine's 2013–14 Euromaidan protests, Russia has consistently sought to discredit Ukrainians as fascists and Nazis and has spread false accusations of the Ukrainian Army committing a genocide against ethnic Russians. On February 24, 2022, the day of Russia's full-scale invasion of Ukraine, Russian President Vladimir Putin used these lies to justify the so-called "special military operation in Ukraine." He also said that Nazism is rife in Lithuania.

These accusations have taken root in some parts of Europe and within Russia's military. In early 2023, I visited an elderly woman at her small farmhouse in a rural part of eastern Ukraine, where she kept bees. She lived on the edge of a small village near Izyum, and told me how, months before, young smiling Russian soldiers had knocked on her door to declare that they had "come to save her from the fascists and Nazis," as though it was 1944.

"I looked at them, a bit confused," she said. "And told them to go home to their mothers, that I didn't need saving from anyone except them. They really thought they were coming to liberate me."

After Russia's February 2022 invasion of Ukraine, the United States and the EU sanctioned Russian state media. Russia-backed channels like RT and Sputnik were blocked from major platforms and lost access to advertising and other financial support, making it harder for the Kremlin's messages to reach Western audiences. In response, Russia stepped up its covert operations: troll farms, fake websites masquerading as legitimate news outlets, and the widespread recruitment of paid influencers to spread propaganda.

In fact, Russia had an extensive online influence operation before the 2022 invasion. An infamous troll farm known as the Internet Research Agency, located in Saint Petersburg, was set up in 2013 and employed as many as nine hundred people two years later. One former troll told *Time* magazine that he earned five thousand rubles a month in 2017—around $700 at the time—a slightly above-average salary in the country. He was expected to produce 135 online commentaries every day, primarily about Ukraine. According to *Time*, "The bosses imposed a few strict rules. First, never be late. Second, never leave early. Third, never criticize President Vladimir Putin online, at least not while on the clock."

According to a researcher on Russia from a Washington, DC, think tank, Russia churns out massive disinformation about Ukraine and the West, "throwing spaghetti at the wall to see what might stick." Many lies go unnoticed, but some have been amplified globally, reaching millions and exploiting audiences' distrust and grievances. For instance, the lurid claim that the United States was secretly developing bioweapons in Ukraine was widely believed. Russian politicians used this as one means to justify the 2022 invasion, and the claim quickly spread worldwide, appearing on both Chinese state media and on Fox News in the United States within a month. Incredibly, a March 2022 YouGov/*Economist* poll found that one in four Americans believed the story.

Much of the disinformation specifically targets Lithuania. In 2017, a false story believed to have come from pro-Kremlin trolls appeared on social media claiming that five NATO soldiers from Germany had raped a teenager in the small city of Jonava in central Lithuania. In 2019, Russian trolls broke into online Lithuanian news platform Kas vyksta Kaune and posted a brazen story about US plans to move nuclear weapons to Lithuania. The story included a fake tweet from then-US Secretary of State Mike Pompeo "congratulating" the Lithuanian president on the news.

In May 2025, rumors were spread across social media that locals living near Lithuania's border with Poland in the Suwalki Gap were fleeing in large numbers because they feared an imminent Russian invasion. These are the typical sorts of disinformation that the Baltic Elves counter by posting their fact-checked truths.

"People can be very stupid, you know?" Giedrius sighed. "As elves, we do what we can to fight this fake news."

The Baltic Elves are not a membership organization. These self-organized volunteers decide when and how much they will work.

"One day you might be active, and the next day not. No one has to be a full-time elf," Giedrius explained. "The elves range from about sixteen to eighty in age, but most are probably middle-aged."

Some elves work on their own, others in teams. Their mission is to debunk fake news. Some specialize in particular themes, and others focus on specific information channels, such as the messaging app Telegram. Others publicly call out pro-Kremlin trolls. It's all part of an enormous effort to keep up with large-scale disinformation campaigns and reclaim the truth.

Giedrius grew up under Soviet occupation as a teenager in the 1980s. His mother was a doctor and his father a university professor of engineering. A self-confessed "nerdy kid, with glasses, not at all sporty," young Giedrius was an avid reader and grew up surrounded by books.

"I read everything possible," he said, "the classics, Tolstoy and Dostoevsky, and so on. And of course I was going to the library, too. But it wasn't possible to read everything I wanted to, because in those days the authorities banned many authors, such as George Orwell, Marcel Proust, and Franz Kafka."

When Giedrius was a child, his grandmother was a strong influence on him. She lived in the city of Kaunas, about seventy miles from Giedrius's home in Vilnius.

"I spent every summer there." He smiled. "I loved it. She lived in an independent Lithuania, before the Second World War, and remembered what life was like before the occupation. She knew what freedom was, and she used to show me books about those days. She trained as a dentist, but times were so difficult that she taught French, too. And her husband, my grandfather, was imprisoned as a political prisoner in the Soviet Vorkuta concentration camps for almost ten years, from 1944 to 1954, even though he wasn't politically active. She had a very tough life, like so many countless others."

When I wanted to know more about his grandmother and asked if it would be okay to include these memories of her in this book, Giedrius choked up a little and said, "Yes, yes, please."

I asked him to write her name in my notebook, so I'd get it right, but even though he spelled it out in capitals, I had to ask him to do it again because his writing was just so awful. He slowly formed "JADVYGA" on the page a second time.

"Yeah, sorry, my writing has always been this bad, since I was at school." Giedrius laughed. "But I got that independent streak from her. It's in my blood. My parents were great, but their attitude was go-along-to-get-along. We were part of the Soviet regime, and we had to accept reality and to make the best of things. My grandmother was much more defiant."

Like other young men in Lithuania, Giedrius was conscripted into the Soviet Army for two years at the age of eighteen.

"That was 1984," recalled Giedrius. "The Russian war against Afghanistan was underway, and so they wanted soldiers. Luckily, I wasn't sent to Afghanistan, but to Saint Petersburg to study at a training center for artillery weapons, learning about repairs and so on. It was a useless time, lost years, really. I spent much of the time working as a carpenter and somehow was appointed as a truck driver of a vehicle I had never even seen."

But things were beginning to change. Even while he was in the army in Saint Petersburg, it was possible to listen to rock music, which had been banned in previous years. The era of perestroika—Mikhail Gorbachev's policy of political and economic reform, which allowed a limited loosening of Soviet repression—was dawning. According to Andrei Kolsenikov, a Russian politics expert, this shift "meant freedom and the emancipation of society from the state for the first time in Russia's entire history."

Although perestroika aimed to revive the stagnating Soviet system, it ultimately helped to bring about its collapse. The economy failed to bounce back. Inflation skyrocketed and shortages deepened. As Moscow loosened its grip, local authorities gained more power, people felt freer to criticize the government, and nationalism surged across the republics. Mass street demonstrations across Eastern Europe in the late 1980s rocked the puppet governments loyal to Russia. At the end of 1989, the Soviet Union suddenly began to teeter and then collapsed. In March 1990, Lithuania became the first country to declare its independence from the Soviet Union, followed by fourteen others in the following years.

"People often ask me, especially those from Western countries, why I bother being an elf, why am I spending time on this when I could be, I don't know"—Giedrius paused, waving a hand around, trying to imagine what anyone who isn't an elf might do with their spare time—"bowling or playing computer games on the weekends," he said finally. "But we lived under occupation for fifty years. Twenty thousand people were killed in the forests fighting for independence, and so this freedom is very important to us. Every family in Lithuania has had a relative killed or sent to Siberia. It's kind of magic that we got our country back, and we have to defend that magic. I don't think everyone in the West understands that."

Giedrius became even more animated talking about democracy.

"Look, this isn't about a stupid Trump version of 'Make Lithuania Great Again.' No, democracy is about values, not just about one country."

And it is mainly across Eastern Europe that the elves have flourished.

"Different countries have different models," said Giedrius. "It's never been like there's one recipe and you have the perfect cake for countering disinformation. It can look very different in different places, but it's the same spirit, the same passion. We don't describe what we do as activism. It's passion. It's about the joy of doing what we feel we should be doing."

Pointing to a nearby table in the café, Giedrius said, "A year ago, I met a guy from Bulgaria just there."

I wondered for a second if I was sitting in the secret elf headquarters.

"He was here traveling with his family," continued Giedrius, "and he asked me about starting up Bulgarian elves. 'How many do we need to start a movement?' and I said, 'One. One elf, an elf with passion. Without the passion for this, just drop it. If you have passion, other people will come. So he went away, and he started up the Bulgarian Elves."

A few years after the Baltic Elves began in Lithuania, some people in the Czech Republic, which had also been under Soviet occupation since the 1940s, saw increasingly orchestrated online disinformation campaigns on a range of issues, including against Ukraine, immigration, and the EU. In 2018, in response to the disinformation, the Czech Elves were born.

Bob Kartous, a media expert and one of two spokespeople for the Czech Elves, told me: "There are hundreds of elves scattered across the country. We're organized in a similar way to the Baltic Elves, in small groups so that any one elf only knows of a few others, and most of those are known only by their nicknames. We've had a few infiltrators, but spotting a fake elf is easy."

Bob estimated that the gender split of the Czech Elves, based on the few he's met, is even, with a typical age range of thirty-five to fifty-five.

"They're all sorts of people—photographers, graphic designers, medical students, IT specialists. Some have a humanities background; others come from careers in security, in the army or police," he said.

Bob credited his interest in disinformation to his formative years as a child around the time of mass street protests at the end of the Soviet Union. As in Lithuania and other countries under Soviet occupation, large-scale pro-democracy demonstrations broke out across Czechoslovakia in late 1989.

"I was twelve when all this was happening," Bob recalled. "I was living in a fairly remote part of the east of the country, far away from the capital of Prague, so news reached us slowly at first. And in spite of Soviet oppression, there was already a sort of passive resistance in my family. My father listened to the Voice of America radio station."

Bob remembered that when the school year began in September 1989, "we started with the usual curriculum, you know, compulsory Russian lessons, and teachers instructing us about the evolution of societies, which developed from capitalism into socialism into the ultimate paradise of communism, and that our society was on the brink of such bliss."

Then in the middle of November came news from Prague of mass demonstrations against the pro-Russian regime. While the uprising looked to be succeeding, with more people protesting every week, there was a nervousness across the country about what would happen next. Giedrius remembered weeks of uncertainty at this time, too, in Lithuania, where similar protests were happening.

For Czechs, there had been a false dawn twenty years earlier. The Prague Spring of early 1968 had delivered some popular reforms, including some freedom for the press to criticize the government. But by August of that same year, when the limited liberalism was proving very popular, the Soviet authorities crushed the movement for reform with troops and tanks.

In 1989, many Czechs feared a repeat.

"Things were changing that winter," recalled Bob, "but it was unclear for quite a while what was going to happen."

I'm around a decade older than Bob, and when I saw the news of the Berlin Wall being crossed and then torn down by protestors, I went to see what was happening for myself. I traveled across Eastern Europe by train in those early weeks of 1990 with a friend, Garry, to see the dramatic history unfolding. We crossed the Berlin Wall and reached Prague. While younger people were keen to talk to us, older people avoided catching our eye or risking a conversation with us. But things were clearly changing. After Lithuania declared independence in March 1990, it became clear the Soviet Union was breaking up.

"School quickly became very different," said Bob. "The same teacher switched from teaching us about communism to giving lessons on liberal democracies, and the compulsory Russian lessons were dropped, replaced with German. I think the teachers were happy about the change."

Bob's childhood under the Soviet system motivated him to fight disinformation. "I have experience of totalitarian regimes, of prohibited works, of banned books. This helped shape my political views."

Czechoslovakia finally ended its relationship with the Soviet Union on the last day of 1992, the culmination of the Velvet Revolution, characterized by a peaceful and smooth transition of power.

Bob remembered those days as "a really euphoric time," marked by a new optimism that was a powerful driving force at the end of the century. "People generally felt like something new was starting, and the future looked really bright, and that euphoria lasted into the mid-'90s. Many people my age are still energized by this formative time period," he said.

But over the last ten years or so, more pessimism about the future, fueled by disinformation, has crept into the public outlook.

Bob said the heady optimism of the first post-Soviet decades has faded, and Russian attacks on European values has found a footing with those becoming disillusioned with the EU and what it provides. So, as with the Baltic Elves, the Czech Elves were created to bring some light to discussions.

The Czech Elves approach their work differently from their Baltic cousins. They don't fight trolls online.

"In our context it doesn't work," explained Bob. "We can't win like that; it's absolutely futile. What works for us is different from what works in Lithuania, or even just next door in Slovakia." Instead, he told me, they provide hard analysis to the local and international journalists and to the government and make persuasive cases to the Czech media about what's true and what's fake.

Bob is also an advisor to the Czech Ministry of Education. The Czech Elves speak with the government and the media about the infrastructure of social media—how it manipulates information and spreads false content—and emphasize the need for user verification to prevent inauthentic accounts from being created.

Another area of their work is speaking out about what Bob referred to as "opportunistic politicians who use disinformation about immigration, about clean energy, to exploit fears. They're commercial fascists, just exploiting these issues without necessarily believing in any ideology except power for themselves."

One project that Bob said helped him "understand more about disinformation and how deeply it gets into people's minds" culminated in a Netflix documentary called *Change My Mind*. He and a film crew took three middle-aged Czech citizens who said they believed Russian propaganda to the eastern front of Russia's war in Ukraine to see how their views could withstand the reality of seeing things for themselves. The two men and one woman insisted there was no real war and that the attacks on Ukrainian towns and cities were fake news. The documentary follows them to Kharkiv, where they see the devastation caused by Russian missiles, and to the mass grave on the outskirts of Izyum.

Over several years, I have extensively documented attacks on Kharkiv, and I have reported on the discovery of the mass grave in the forest at Izyum, where at least four hundred civilians were found buried after Russian soldiers left in 2022. I know firsthand how shocking it is to see these places.

The documentary was an ingenious project, confronting credulous believers of disinformation with the sobering reality they denied. And yet in spite of seeing the evidence for themselves, none of the three was able to see the bigger picture.

"They admitted that there was a war happening after all," said Bob, "but still blamed the West for it. It was too important to their identities to change their minds—they had to keep their views on what was happening in Ukraine, or it would mean questioning their whole belief systems."

The documentary hit a nerve in the Czech Republic, sparking a widespread debate about why people choose not to believe the truth and whether they can change their views. It's also another example of how elves operate differently across different borders and cultures. An initiative by the EU to coordinate elves from a dozen different countries "didn't really take off," said Bob. "The contexts were too different."

While elves across Europe face different local challenges, one force that may potentially affect their work across the board is artificial intelligence (AI). Bob's views on the threats of AI are different from those of Giedrius. Along with the threats, Bob pointed to possible positive impacts for the development of critical thinking when used adequately in education.

The US-based think tank Atlantic Council has warned that AI "reduces the financial cost, time, and technical expertise required to produce mass amounts of hyperrealistic, harmful content and potentially spread it at scale." NewsGuard, an organization that monitors misinformation, has identified networks of AI-generated websites designed to flood the internet with falsehoods and even shape the responses produced by leading chatbots—in some cases, with measurable success.

By contrast, Giedrius doesn't see AI as such a looming danger. "AI can't help idiots." He laughed. "If we use it the way we use smartphones, in an intelligent way, it won't be a danger. There's always some new magical thing that comes along and scares everyone. AI will come, and we will be okay."

Similarly, apocalyptic predictions had been made about how the rise of technology would destroy more jobs than it created and how texting would kill language. (The opposite is true in both cases.)

"AI won't be the end of civilization," Giedrius said. "It's like when the Gutenberg printing press was perfected in 1450. People were probably moaning about that, you know, in the years that followed."

Giedrius mimicked a grumpy, shaky voice and wagged a trembling finger: "'Look at all those young people reading newly accessible material, not talking to us. They'll spend the rest of their lives looking down into their books and ignoring their neighbors, and this will be the end of society.'"

In Giedrius's view, more important than developing software to identify AI-generated disinformation is training people in media literacy, the better to assess all sources of information critically. Schoolchildren are taught this at an early age in Finland, he said approvingly, and this is where energy should be spent. Finland consistently ranks first on the European Media Literacy Index, which compares countries' "resilience against disinformation."

Apart from countering disinformation, the Baltic Elves have also taken their campaigns to big brands, including Adidas and Walmart, which were selling products the elves saw as glorifying the former Soviet Union.

"Before the 2018 football World Cup, the elves noticed that Adidas was selling shirts and jerseys with CCCP [the Russian initials for the USSR, the Soviet regime] across the front," said Giedrius. This attempt at commercializing vintage communist chic went down badly in the Baltics, where memories of Soviet occupation were extremely painful. Lithuania's Ministry of Foreign Affairs criticized Adidas for promoting "imperial nostalgia." The elves took to social media and joined others in an international campaign to have the merchandise stopped, and within days Adidas stopped selling the jerseys.

"Then the elves saw that Walmart was selling children's clothes with the hammer-and-sickle Communist logo," Giedrius said. "In the Baltics, this is obviously associated with the Soviet occupation. I mean, what's next—swastikas?" Giedrius complained to the US media about the glorification of the logo. "I did a TV interview, and the next day it was on American news from Alaska to Washington, DC."

The campaign took off, and Lithuania's then-Ambassador to the United States Rolandas Kriščiūnas 'sent an open letter to the company's leadership calling for the removal of any products with Soviet imagery. Politicians from other Eastern European countries joined the call, and Walmart soon withdrew the products.

"That was a successful operation," said Giedrius. "But you have to be ready and able to fight propaganda on all sorts of fronts. Disinformation is doing serious damage across the globe. Look at America. Disinformation and disagreement about 'facts' sometimes seems to have brought the country to the edge of a civil war." But despite these constant distortions of the truth, Giedrius said he is "a chronic optimist. That's my strength and my weakness. I do believe that we will be winners one day, but I don't know which day exactly."

Giedrius was born a few years after me, and we have much the same historical memory. We agree that for those whose memories don't reach back to the 1970s or 1980s, the world can seem irrevocably locked in a doomed downward spiral. For those of us who can recall life before then, things still look grim, but they're not necessarily doomed.

"Look at the terrorism of the 1970s across Europe," Giedrius said. "The Red Army Faction in Germany, the Red Brigades in Italy. Look at how terrible things were in Northern Ireland then."

We talked about the 1970s and 1980s, when the racist apartheid regime governed South Africa, when much of Latin America was ruled by military dictatorships, when in Europe the military generals were in charge in Spain and Greece and, of course, the Soviet Union occupied the Baltics and all of Eastern Europe. Our experience leads us to share a view of history across decades and to discuss how to avoid the mistakes of the past. We talked about Brexit and what Britain's withdrawal from Europe might mean, as Giedrius spent some time living in England when newly independent Lithuania encouraged its young professionals to learn more about other countries.

We moved on to Western Europe's slow response to the latest wave of Russian imperialism, and the relevance today of the young John F. Kennedy's 1939 undergraduate thesis *Why England Slept,* which outlined why Western democracies were slow to prepare for the threat of war from Nazi Germany.

"As I've said, I'm positive about the future," said Giedrius. "I've started to write articles, which is sort of funny and magical because I was always so bad at writing at school. I'm writing a piece saying Putin is really failing because he is uniting Western Europe against him. Things that were unimaginable a few years ago are happening because of him—Finland and Sweden joining NATO, and most of the world supporting Ukraine against him. Putin is the biggest loser in modern Russian history."

Giedrius took a final sip of his coffee. It was time for us to part.

"I hate war," Giedrius said as we stood. "Nothing is more terrible. But when we have to, we fight. You have to show you're strong. It's like on the street: If you show hooligans you're weak, they will attack you." He continued while he put on his coat: "For me, the European Union is one of the most magical things ever, and we have to fight to keep it, and not just sit back when there is this torrent of disinformation. Our main idea is: If you do nothing, it always adds up to zero, but if you do something, it could be 1 percent successful or 100 percent successful. Whatever it is, it's still a plus. It's not zero."

ACKNOWLEDGMENTS

The first time I met Tracy Aanenson in person, we talked about all sorts of things over coffee, including how human rights language often is off-putting, over professionalized, and trapped in a legal vocabulary, and how everyday people doing good things are overlooked and uncelebrated. She explained how she was setting up Humanitas Media to tell individual stories in a relatable way, partly to show people what others are doing.

By the end of our talk, we had conceived the idea of a book based on the theme of kindness in action, and I agreed to deliver a manuscript nine months later.

A labor of love, this required finding a variety of people motivated by kindness doing different work in different locations, and ideally without professional human rights experience. The idea was to show that doing great things doesn't depend on qualifications or experience.

I had some people to profile in mind already, but I put the word out to friends and colleagues, asking for more ideas. I owe much to Fiachra Bourke, Lorena Cotza, Rebecca Everly, Patty Evers, Mary Lawlor, Michael Phoenix, Madeline Roache, and Suchita Uppal for their suggestions and introductions to those I profiled.

My thanks, too, to Madeline Roache for her ruthlessly enthusiastic editing, to Allen Peacock for his experienced eye and advice on the copy. Mikola De Roo and Jeremy Townsend further refined the text, and I want to thank them and Rick Lebo, too, for the maps.

Jacqui Daniels at Humanitas Media is a wonderful colleague, and I am very grateful for her skilled promotion and marketing of the book. Sara Anani proved an excellent interpreter and translator, and I thank her for her patience and cheerful professionalism. My thanks, too, to gifted photographer Gayane Malakyan for taking the jacket photo of me on a cold day in Kyiv.

This book couldn't have happened without the generosity of those I interviewed, giving me their time to share their stories with me, and then more time checking to be sure that what I'd written about them was accurate. I'm deeply grateful to them. Any remaining mistakes are mine.

My last thanks goes again to Tracy Aanenson for creating Humanitas Media, for believing this project was possible, and for enabling it to happen.

ENDNOTES

Introduction:

x He was detained for weeks: Ela Yokes, "How Sudanese Rights Defenders Are Risking Their Lives to Document the War," *New Humanitarian,* March 11, 2024, https://www.thenewhumanitarian.org/feature/2024/03/11/sudan-how-sudanese-rights-defenders-are-risking-their-lives-document-war.

xi In Northern Ireland, she became an "accidental activist": Ronan McSherry and Martin McGuinness, hosts, *TwoMacs Podcast,* episode 40, part 2, "Bernadette Devlin McAliskey," April 7, 2025, 1 hr., 12 min., https://twomacs.buzzsprout.com/2209034/episodes/16932731-twomacs-podcast-bernadette-devlin-mcaliskey-ep-40-part2.

xvi East German gas station attendants: Anna Funder, *Stasiland: Stories from Behind the Berlin Wall* (Granta, 2003), 63.

xvi Halik Kochanski recounts an incident in Warsaw: Halik Kochanski, *Resistance: The Underground War in Europe, 1939–1945* (Allen Lane, 2022), xvii.

xvi We can trace this thread of nonviolent defiance: For centuries some who were not so nonviolent have also captured popular imagination in Europe and beyond, mythologized and adored for their refusal to compromise on justice. From Spartacus to Robin Hood to William Tell, it is these resistance heroes who are celebrated across generations for their daring acts of dissent, not the emperors and kings and presidents who oppressed them.

Take Spartacus, the gladiator who led a slave revolt against Rome in 73 B.C.E. Breaking out of the gladiator barracks at Capua with seventy-three others, he marched up and down the length of Italy, amassing an army of tens of thousands of renegades and runaway slaves that threatened the most powerful empire in the world for two years. Roman soldiers commanded by General Marcus Licinius Crassus eventually killed Spartacus on the battlefield at Silarus. But historian Barry Strauss in *The Spartacus War* (Weidenfeld & Nicholson, 2009) details how for years afterward, slaves blessed Spartacus's memory, keeping it alive, musing that "Spartacus was a failure against Rome but a success as a mythmaker. . . . Who, today, remembers Crassus?" See also Michael Rosen and David Widgery, *The Chatto Book of Dissent* (Chatto, 1991), 4. Or consider Robin Hood, another legendary figure, whose popularity has endured since the thirteenth century in dozens of ballads, movies, and countless books as a symbol of justice. Similar versions of this story surface in other cultures—such as Switzerland's William Tell, and Russia's *Dubrovsky,* an infuriatingly unfinished 1832 novel by Alexander Pushkin in *Notes, Tales, Journeys* (Penguin, 2016), 127.

xvi A man named Charles Cunningham Boycott: Bernard Becker, *Disturbed Ireland* (Macmillan, 1881), 17. Jean Bruller's 1941 French novel *Le silence de la mer,* translated by Cyril Connolly *The Silence of the Sea* (Macmillan, 1944), tells the story of a man and his niece who are forced to house a German officer during the occupation of France. In a powerful echo of the mental resistance and ostracization of the original boycott, the pair simply refuse to acknowledge him or talk to him.

xvii a courageous twenty-two-year-old East German student: Helena Merriman, *Tunnel 29* (Hodder & Stoughton, 2022), 86.

xviii The youths eventually helped dozens of people to escape to the West: Merriman, *Tunnel 29*.

xviii "resistance was a spontaneous reaction to oppression": Kochanski, *Resistance:* 828, quoted in Douglas Dodds-Parker, *Setting Europe Ablaze: Some Accounts of Ungentlemanly Warfare* (Springwood Books, 1983), 3.

xviii Others echoed the famed French Resistance activist: Margaret Collins Weitz, *Sisters in the Resistance: How Women Fought to Free France, 1940–1945* (John Wiley, 1995), 9. For a discussion of what constituted resistance, see page 8. For more on resistance to Nazism from within Germany, see German novelist Irmgard Keun's series of books mocking the rise of the Nazi Party in the 1930s, including the *Artificial Silk Girl* (1932) and *After Midnight* (1937). Seeing Keun's popular novels as a threat to their dictatorship, the Nazis banned them. Hans Fallad's 1947 book *Alone in Berlin*, adapted into a 2016 movie, tells the true story of middle-aged married Berlin couple Otto and Anna Quangel: Starting in 1940, they left anonymous postcards criticizing Hitler all over Germany's capital for three years before being caught and executed.

xix "Were they oddballs and eccentrics or idealists": Robert Gildea, *Fighters in the Shadows: A New History of the French Resistance* (Faber and Faber, 2015), 16. In *Army of Shadows*, a 1943 work about the French Resistance—one of the first written of the organization—Joseph Kessel declared that "the national hero is the clandestine man, the outlaw."

xix "But I must honestly say": Dr. Martin Luther King Jr., speech at Southern Methodist University, March 17, 1966, https://www.smu.edu/news/archives/2014/mlk-at-smu-transcript-17march1966.

xx "Expectations that defenders were strong": Alice M. Nah, ed., *Protecting Human Rights Defenders at Risk* (Routledge, 2020).

xx–xxi "Those who took part in the resistance were not supermen": Kochanski, *Resistance,* xxi.

xxi "Let's face it," he said to me over coffee: Brian Dooley, Gulf Centre for Human Rights, "Ahmed Mansoor: Isolated but Not Alone," IFEX, May 29, 2019, https://ifex.org/ahmed-mansoor-isolated-but-not-alone/.

xxi Margaret Mead is often quoted: Despite widespread use of the "Never doubt" quote, there is no documentation for where or when Mead said it. Another variation also attributed to Mead is "Never believe that a few caring people can't change the world. For indeed that's all who ever have."

xxii Eighteenth-century Irish Philosopher:
Edmund Burke, "Thoughts on the Cause of the Present Discontents" 82-83 (1770) in*Select Works of Edmund Burke,* vol. 1, p. 146 (Liberty Fund ed. 1999).

Chapter 1:
11 Six people were found dead in the rubble: Asami Terajimi, "Update: Russian Missile Attack on Kharkiv Kills Six People, Including Three-Year-Old Child, Injures at Least Thirty-One," *Kyiv Independent,* January 4, 2026, https://kyivindependent.com/russian-attack-on-kharkiv-injures-at-least-15-people-including-a-baby-local-authorities-report/.

Chapter 2:
14 As soon as it landed, the police stormed the plane: Olga Loginova, "A Fake Ryanair Hijack—and the Fear That Has Stalked Belarus's People Ever Since," *Guardian,* October 19, 2023, https://www.theguardian.com/global-development/2023/oct/19/a-fake-ryanair-hijack-and-the-fear-that-has-stalked-belaruss-people-ever-since.

15 *Many desperate refugees are crammed onto dangerous boats:* "Ten Years Since the Largest Loss of Life in the Mediterranean, UNHCR Urges Decisive Action to Save Lives" (press release), UNHCR, April 17, 2025, https://www.unhcr.org/europe/news/press-releases/10-years-largest-loss-life-mediterranean-unhcr-urges-decisive-action-save-lives.

16 *A BBC news report revealed the use of tear gas:* "Poland Border Crisis: Scenes of Chaos as Soldiers Deploy Water Cannon," BBC News, November 16, 2021, video, 1 min., 45 sec., https://www.bbc.co.uk/news/av/world-europe-59307350. Other people said the Polish guards had been kinder and provided them with food, water, and clothing; see "Violence and Pushbacks at Poland–Belarus Border," Human Rights Watch, June 7, 2022, https://www.hrw.org/news/2022/06/07/violence-and-pushbacks-poland-belarus-border.

16 *One man drowned:* "Belarus/EU: New Evidence of Brutal Violence from Belarusian Forces Against Asylum Seekers and Migrants Facing Pushbacks from the EU," Amnesty International, December 21, 2021, https://www.amnesty.org/en/latest/news/2021/12/belarus-eu-new-evidence-of-brutal-violence-from-belarusian-forces-against-asylum-seekers-and-migrants-facing-pushbacks-from-the-eu/.

16 *stopping one hundred thousand attempted crossings:* Deutsche Welle, "Poland, Baltics Step Up Border Controls Amid Migrant Crisis," InfoMigrants, June 17, 2024, https://www.infomigrants.net/en/post/57794/poland-baltics-step-up-border-controls-amid-migrant-crisis.

22 *Since September 2021, over a hundred people have died:* "Interactive Dashboards" (data on the Poland–Belarus border), We Are Monitoring,https://wearemonitoring.org.pl/en/list-of-the-deceased/. UN IOM Stats at least 130 people dead or missing along the Belarus-EU border https://missingmigrants.iom.int/region/europe. See also "Poland: Brutal Pushbacks at Belarus Border," Human Rights Watch, December 10, 2024, https://www.hrw.org/news/2024/12/10/poland-brutal-pushbacks-belarus-border.

25 ***human rights activist Ieva Raubiško was convicted:*** "We Don't Want a World Where People Are Afraid to Help Each Other: Joint Statement of Support for Ieva Raubiško," Helsinki Foundation for Human Rights, May 21, 2024, https://hfhr.pl/en/news/support-ieva-raubisko.

27 ***"The ideal subject of totalitarian rule":*** Tatjana Tömmel and Maurizio Passerin d'Entrèves, "Hannah Arendt," *Stanford Encyclopedia of Philosophy* (Spring 2025 edition), eds. Edward N. Zalta and Uri Nodelman, https://plato.stanford.edu/archives/spr2025/entries/arendt/. See also Hannah Arendt, *The Origins of Totalitarianism,* New Edition (Harvest, 1973), 473, https://archive.org/details/hannah-arendt-the-origins-of-totalitarianism/page/n5/mode/2up?q=%22the+ideal+subject+of+totalitarian+rule%22.

27 ***Accepting his 1970 Nobel Prize for Literature:*** Aleksandr Solzhenitsyn, "Nobel Lecture," [1972], trans. Alexis Klimoff, Aleksandr Solzhenitsyn Center, https://www.solzhenitsyncenter.org/nobel-lecture. From *The Solzhenitsyn Reader,* trans. Alexis Klimoff (Harper & Row, 1980).

Chapter 3:

35 ***According to the World Health Organization:*** https://www.who.int/news-room/fact-sheets/detail/cancer#:~:text=Key%20facts,lower%2Dmiddle%2Dincome%20countries.

36 ***International academic studies show:*** https://pmc.ncbi.nlm.nih.gov/articles/PMC2515569/#:~:text=Only%205%E2%80%9310%25%20of%20all,in%20the%20environment%20and%20lifestyle.

44 ***Weeks later, six hundred academics:*** "Open Letter in Support of Dr. Bülent Şık, Sentenced to Prison for Publicizing Threats to Public Health," July 10, 2020, https://docs.google.com/forms/d/e/1FAIpQLSc6dYFX1VL-2N-TyC4R-wthVY5CcHYO93TMs10JvIt4otHtYg/viewform. Earlier version available via the International

Association of Health Policy, February 24, 2020, https://iahponline.org/2020/02/24/open-letter-in-support-of-dr-bulent-sik-sentenced-to-prison-for-publicizing-threats-to-public-health/. https://bianet.org/haber/academics-scientists-launch-petition-for-dr-bulent-sik-demand-his-conviction-overturned-220417

45 ***Paris-based NGO Reporters Without Borders said:*** "Turkish Public Health Whistleblower Sentenced to Fifteen Months in Jail," Reporters Without Borders (RSF), September 27, 2019, https://rsf.org/en/turkish-public-health-whistleblower-sentenced-15-months-jail.

Chapter 4:

47 ***Wednesday night, December 9, 2015:*** "December 9, 2015: Weather History in Prague," Weather Spark, December 9, 2015, https://weatherspark.com/h/d/77807/2015/12/9/Historical-Weather-on-Wednesday-December-9-2015-in-Prague-Czechia#Figures-Temperature.

47 ***Sixty-three percent of people in the Czech Republic:*** Ruth Fraňková, "Amnesty International: Seven Thousand Women Raped in Czech Republic Every Year," Radio Prague International, September 23, 2015, https://english.radio.cz/amnesty-international-7000-women-raped-czech-republic-every-year-8247446.

48 ***The UN estimates that one in three women:*** "Global Database on Violence Against Women and Girls," 2009–present, UN Women, https://data.unwomen.org/global-database-on-violence-against-women, accessed March 24, 2026.

49 ***While I was working for Amnesty International:*** https://www.theguardian.com/uk/2005/nov/21/ukcrime.prisonsandprobation#:~:text=One%20in%20three%20people%20believes,one%20in%20three%20in%201977.

52 ***The film shows a man talking to his friend:*** "Rande na Valentýna je super, znásilnění ne! Když to nechce, tak to nechceš" ("A Valentine's

Day Date Is Great, but Rape Is Not! If She Doesn't Want it, You Don't Want It"), created by Konsent, posted February 3, 2021, by YouTube, 34 sec., https://youtu.be/6WOt3oAaoz8.

55 ***After years of public protests, in 2023, Konsent:*** Jules Eisenchteter, "Czech Government Prepares New Legal Definition of Rape," Balkan Insight, June 5, 2023, https://balkaninsight.com/2023/06/05/czech-government-prepares-new-legal-definition-of-rape/.

55 ***In recent years, twelve other European countries:*** Tim Gosling, "Czechia Tested by Its #MeToo Moment," Balkan Insight, July 26, 2023, https://balkaninsight.com/2021/07/26/czechia-tested-by-its-metoo-moment/.

56 ***Younger men across the world:*** Jonathan Yerushalmy, "What's Behind the Global Political Divide between Young Men and Women?," *Guardian*, November 13, 2024, https://www.theguardian.com/us-news/2024/nov/14/us-election-donald-trump-voters-gender-race-data. See also John Burn-Murdoch, "A New Global Gender Divide Is Emerging," *Financial Times*, January 25, 2024, https://www.ft.com/content/29fd9b5c-2f35-41bf-9d4c-994db4e12998.

56 ***Online, men are turning to extreme communities:*** Manoel Horta Ribeiro, Jeremy Blackburn, Barry Bradlyn, Emiliano De Cristofaro, Gianluca Stringhini, Summer Long, Stephanie Greenberg, and Savvas Zannettou, "The Evolution of the Manosphere across the Web," *Proceedings of the International AAAI Conference on Web and Social Media*, 15 (1; 2021), 196–207, https://doi.org/10.1609/icwsm.v15i1.18053.

57 ***Amnesty International calls it "the gold standard":*** "Here's Why the Istanbul Convention Saves Lives," Amnesty International, May 7, 2021, https://www.amnesty.org/en/latest/news/2021/05/heres-why-the-istanbul-convention-saves-lives/.

57 ***the Istanbul Convention, a Council of Europe agreement:*** Council of Europe Convention on Preventing and Combating Violence Against

Women and Domestic Violence, Council of Europe [aka the Istanbul Convention], April 12, 2011, https://rm.coe.int/168046031c.

Chapter 5:

64 Hill admitted to the murder of Brian Shaw: Ric Clark, "Twenty Years of Pain for IRA Victim's Family," UPI, February 22, 1994, https://www.upi.com/Archives/1994/02/22/Twenty-years-of-pain-for-IRA-victims-family/5262761893200/.

64 Armstrong later recalled his feelings: Paddy Armstrong with Mary-Elaine Tynan, *Life after Life: A Guildford Four Memoir* (Gill Books, 2017).

69 Logan privately told another lawyer: Ros Franey and Grant McKee, eds., *Time Bomb: Irish Bombers, English Justice and the Guildford Four* (Muswell Press, 2024).

Chapter 6:

82 Yanukovych stated that the six-thousand-hectare forest: "Yanukovych Instructed the Heads of the Kyiv City State Administration and the Kyiv Regional State Administration to Take Measures to Preserve the Bilychansky Forest," PenoptepUA, March 2, 2012, https://reporter-ua.com/2012/03/02/yanukovich-poruchil-predsedatelyam-kgga-i-koga-prinyat-mery-dlya-sohraneniya.

83 For decades, Ukrainians have seen oligarchic power: "Ukrainians See Corruption and Oligarchs as Greatest Threat to Their Country," Ukrinform, October 3, 2017, https://www.ukrinform.net/rubric-society/2317493-ukrainians-see-corruption-and-oligarchs-as-greatest-threat-to-their-country.html.

83 In 2008, Ukraine ranked 134th out of 180: "Stark Warnings from Transparency International," Human Rights in Ukraine, September 23, 2008, https://khpg.org/en/1222174179.

83 *Activists, journalists, and officials who oppose the oligarchs:* "Kateryna Handzyuk: Ukrainian Anti-Corruption Activist Dies After Acid Attack," *Independent,* November 5, 2018, https://www.independent.co.uk/news/world/europe/kateryna-handzyuk-dead-ukraine-acid-attack-corruption-activist-campaigner-a8617846.html. See also "101 Incidents of Persecution of Activists Recorded in Ukraine Last Year," Human Rights Center ZMINA, January 29, 2021, https://zmina.ua/en/event-en/101-incidents-of-persecution-of-activists-recorded-in-ukraine-last-year/ and "Persecution of Anti-Corruption Activists Must Stop in Ukraine," Transparency International, November 13, 2017, https://www.transparency.org/en/press/persecution-of-anti-corruption-activists-must-stop-in-ukraine.

93 *"We are all fighting together":* "Holka: Building a Network of Activists across Ukraine to Fight Corruption," European Endowment for Democracy, March 6, 2025, https://democracyendowment.eu/stories/holka.

Chapter 7:

98 *More than one million people have taken this route:* "Western Balkans Route," European Council/ Council of the European Union, updated March 4, 2025, https://www.consilium.europa.eu/en/policies/western-balkans-route/. See also William Spindler, "2015: The Year of Europe's Refugee Crisis," UNHCR, December 8, 2015, https://www.unhcr.org/uk/news/stories/2015-year-europes-refugee-crisis.

99 *At least four hundred migrants have died:* Laura Lungarotti and Joanie Durocher, "The End Game: Risking Everything on the Western Balkans Route," *Forced Migration Review 75 (May 2025),* https://www.fmreview.org/dangerous-journeys/lungarotti-durocher/.

104 *According to the World Bank:* https://www.worldbank.org/en/news/press-release/2024/10/31/1-2-billion-people-at-high-risk-from-climate-change-worldwide#:~:text=According%20to%20the%20

World%20Bank%20Group%2C%201.2,to%20each%20country's%20specific%20situation%20is%20important.

106 Soon after, the charges were dropped: "Investigation against Migrant Rights Defenders Lorena Fornasir and Gian Andrea Franchi Closed," November 30, 2021, Front Line Defenders, https://www.frontlinedefenders.org/en/case/investigation-against-migrant-rights-defenders-lorena-fornasir-and-gian-andrea-franchi-closed.

Chapter 8:

110 The region had been recognized as an area of outstanding natural beauty: "Sperrin Area of Outstanding Natural Beauty," Northern Ireland Department of Agriculture, Environment and Rural Affairs, https://www.daera-ni.gov.uk/articles/sperrin-area-outstanding-natural-beauty.

111 It's an issue I've researched and written about: Brian Dooley, *Black and Green: Civil Rights Struggles in Northern Ireland and Black America* (Pluto Press, 1998).

111 An increasing amount of evidence is emerging: International Expert Panel: Dr. Brian Dooley, Dr. Aoife Duffy, María José Guembe, Kjell Erik Eriksen, and Ron Dudai, "Bitter Legacy: State Impunity in the Northern Ireland Conflict," Norwegian Center for Human Rights, University of Oslo, April 29, 2024, https://www.jus.uio.no/smr/english/about/id/law/nipanel.html.

111 Overall, an estimated 3,720 people were killed: International Expert Panel, "Bitter Legacy," 10. See also "Report Reveals State Impunity in Northern Ireland Conflict," Norwegian Center for Human Rights, University of Oslo, April 29, 2024, https://www.jus.uio.no/smr/english/about/id/news/2024/report-reveals-state-impunity-in-northern-ireland-.html.

112 They also warn that the air will be contaminated: "Save Our Sperrins (SOS) Campaign Takes Message to London," *Ireland Live,*

December 4, 2025, https://www.ireland-live.ie/news/derry-now/1959827/save-our-sperrins-sos-campaign-takes-message-to-london.html.

112 "The mountains support farming, ecotourism: Save Our Sperrins, *The Sperrins Podcast,* season 1, episode 1, "Introduction to Save Our Sperrins Podcast," Podbean, January 11, 2025, 5 min., 1 sec., https://buttonsoptions4u.podbean.com/e/introduction-to-sperrins-podcast/.

115 A thirty-eight-year-old mother of five children: Garrett Hargan, "We Will Fight On for Answers, Says Son of Pregnant Tyrone Mum Murdered by UVF in 1994," *Belfast Telegraph,* August 3, 2024, https://www.belfasttelegraph.co.uk/news/northern-ireland/we-will-fight-on-for-answers-says-son-of-pregnant-tyrone-mum-murdered-by-uvf-in-1994/a168229705.html.

116 Eamonn McDevitt, a twenty-eight-year-old: "Apology Call over Killing of Eamon McDevitt in Strabane in 1971," BBC News, August 18, 2021, https://www.bbc.co.uk/news/uk-northern-ireland-foyle-west-58262059.

118 the site could produce one hundred metric tons of gold: Julian Fowler, "The Controversial Gold Mine Set to Go before a Planning Inquiry," BBC News, January 10, 2025, https://www.bbc.com/news/articles/ce323x20x3go.

119 granted Dalradian a Discharge Consent: "Fidelma O'Kane," extraORDINARYwomen, Linen Hall Library, Northern Ireland Political Collection, https://www.extraordinarywomenni.com/collections/archives/nipcoka.

121 There was a BBC Northern Ireland Spotlight TV documentary: BBC One, "Gold Rush, The War in the Sperrins," October 26, 2021, https://www.bbc.co.uk/programmes/m001120j. Lyndsey Telford, "War in the Sperrins, Spotlight NI 26-10-2021," created by Dontmineus, posted October 26, 2021, YouTube, 46 min., 22 sec., https://youtu.be/MLPLAZdhSjM.

122 ***He showed me an adjacent field:*** Peadar O'Cearnaigh, "A Single Protester Stops a Gold Mining Company from Drilling After Chaining Himself to Its Equipment," *Canary*, January 22, 2019, https://www.thecanary.co/uk/2019/01/21/a-single-protester-stops-a-gold-mining-company-from-drilling-after-chaining-himself-to-its-equipment.

122 ***Cormac's protest generated more publicity:*** Suzanne McGonagle, "Campaigner Chains Himself to Drill Rig at the Site of a Proposed Gold Mine in Co Tyrone," *Irish News*, January 21, 2019, https://www.irishnews.com/news/northernirelandnews/2019/01/21/news/campaigner-chains-himself-to-drill-rig-at-the-site-of-a-proposed-gold-mine-in-co-tyrone-1532217/.

122 ***Although Cormac was not arrested or charged:*** "Sperrins Gold Mine: Campaigner 'Shocked' by Arrest," BBC, January 24, 2019, https://www.bbc.co.uk/news/uk-northern-ireland-46984409. See also "Goldmining Campaigner Charged," *Irish News*, July 31, 2019, https://www.irishnews.com/news/northernirelandnews/2019/07/31/news/goldmining-campaigner-charged-1674106/.

123 ***Fidelma and Cormac have also visited London twice:*** Save Our Sperrins (@SaveOurSperrins), "Day One of Our #DalradianOut Trip to London City," Facebook, December 2, 2021, https://www.facebook.com/SaveOurSperrins/posts/1588871651448997. See also Save Our Sperrins(@SaveOurSperrins), "Day Two of Our #DalradianOut Trip to London City," Facebook, December 3, 2021, https://www.facebook.com/SaveOurSperrins/posts/1589525851383577; and Save Our Sperrins (@SaveOurSperrins), "Thanks to Colum Eastwood MP for Hosting a Delegation from Save Our Sperrins at Westminster," Facebook, December 5, 2025, https://www.facebook.com/SaveOurSperrins/posts/pfbid02BnjSPPqzuojcGJQpcgeSEm6RAcEZZno56LxwFxNh159Qn5YoxunLemDYNGQ8mjwGl.

123 ***Mary Lawlor spoke at a 2025 event:*** "Save Our Sperrins Celebrates Ten Years & Experts Confirm the Law Is on Our Side," Save

Our Sperrins, July 28, 2025, https://dontmineus.com/what-would-our-great-great-great-great-grandchildren-say-about-goldmining/.

123 brought "not just international recognition, but dignity": "HRDs, Climate Change, and a Just Transition —Guest Blog from Save Our Sperrins," US Special Rapporteur on Human Rights Defenders, September 16, 2025, https://srdefenders.org/information/hrds-climate-change-guest-blog-save-our-sperrins/.

123 "What started as a quiet planning application": "HRDs, Climate Change, and a Just Transition."

123 Their public criticism was widely seen as a message: John Breslin, "US Congressmen Send Warning Letter Linking Long Delayed Co Tyrone Gold Mine to Wider Investor Confidence in Northern Ireland," *Irish News,* May 25, 2025, https://www.irishnews.com/news/northern-ireland/us-congressmen-send-warning-letter-linking-long-delayed-co-tyrone-gold-mine-to-wider-investor-confidence-in-northern-ireland-3BEF74WDEJCMXMABNJW2BBMKIQ/.

124 "Bureaucracy must not become a barrier to progress": Jonathan McCambridge, "Delays over Gold Mine Project Harming NI's Reputation, US Ambassador Warns," PA Media, November 19, 2025, https://uk.news.yahoo.com/delays-over-gold-mine-project-185357604.html.

Chapter 9:

128 A study published in 2025 found suicide rates had risen: Chad D. Meyerhoefer, Bingjin Xue, and Anna Poznańska, "Implications of the Decline in LGBT Rights for Population Mental Health: Evidence from Polish 'LGBT-Free Zones,'" *Journal of Health Economics,* 100 (March 2025), https://doi.org/10.1016/j.jhealeco.2025.102973.

134 Paweł's technical skills turned the data in Kuba's spreadsheets: Atlas of Hate, https://atlasnienawisci.pl/.

138 ***The European Commission President:*** https://www.theguardian.com/world/2020/sep/16/ursula-von-der-leyen-says-polands-lgbt-free-zones-have-no-place-in-eu#:~:text=5%20years%20old-,Ursula%20von%20der%20Leyen%20says%20Poland's%20'LGBT%2Dfree%20zones',no%20place%20in%20our%20union.%E2%80%9D

139 ***they won a host of national and international awards:*** Awards included Soul of Stonewall Award, presented by the Berlin Pride Parade Committee; Premio MADO, awarded by the Madrid Gay Pride Parade Committee; City of Paris International Prize for LGBTQ+ Rights, awarded by the Paris City Hall; POLCUL Award, granted by the Father Adam Boniecki Foundation; Crown of Equality, awarded by the KPH; (Campaign Against Homophobia), organized by the Empower Beyond Foundation/? https://www.lgbtdiamondsawards.pl/en and the nomination for the Sakharov Prize, awarded by the European Parliament.

140 ***"When we started, we didn't think about winning":*** https://blog.atlasnienawisci.pl/index.php/2025/04/24/wszystkie-uchwaly-anty-lgbt-uchylone/

Chapter 10:

144 ***While these industries have long been the backbone:*** Vladimir Berbatović, "Coal Plant Kakanj in BiH Halts Electricity Production amid Record Air Pollution," Balkan Green Energy News, November 18, 2025, https://balkangreenenergynews.com/coal-plant-kakanj-in-bih-halts-electricity-production-amid-record-air-pollution/.

144 ***Bosnia produces two-thirds of its electricity from coal:*** "In Bosnia, the Path to Renewables Runs through Its Coal Mines," November 28, 2024, France 24, https://www.france24.com/en/live-news/20241128-in-bosnia-the-path-to-renewables-runs-through-its-coal-mines.

144 ***The Bosnian capital of Sarajevo is ranked:*** https://www.iqair.com/sa/newsroom/december-3-2025-sarajevo-among-top-10-most-polluted-cities-in-the-world

145 ***Yugoslavia had united six republics:*** Jessica Bateman, "'Everyone Loved Each Other': The Rise of Yugonostalgia," *Guardian,* August 25, 2022, https://www.theguardian.com/world/2022/aug/25/everyone-loved-each-other-rise-yugonostalgia-tito.

146 ***a brutal campaign of ethnic cleansing:*** "Bosnia and Herzegovina," United States Holocaust Memorial Museum, https://www.ushmm.org/genocide-prevention/countries/bosnia-herzegovina.

147 ***The US-brokered Dayton Accords split Bosnia***: Martin Walker, "No War Crimes Deal, Vows US," *Guardian,* November 2, 1995, https://www.theguardian.com/world/from-the-archive-blog/2020/nov/18/the-dayton-accords-a-peace-agreement-for-bosnia-archive-1995.

149 ***These metals were intended to be shipped:*** "Mining Sparks Revival in Bosnia's Vareš," Connecting the Region, January 29, 2025, https://connectingregion.com/news/mining-sparks-revival-in-bosnias-vares.

151 ***But a December 2025 news report revealed:*** "We Contacted the Vareš Health Center: Details about the Presence of Lead in the Blood of Residents Have Been Published," Radio Sarajevo, December 18, 2025, https://radiosarajevo.ba/vijesti/bosna-i-hercegovina/kontaktirali-smo-dom-zdravlja-vares-objavljeni-detalji-o-prisustvu-olova-u-krvi-stanovnika/618576. See also Fojničani Civic Association, "Lead Found in the Blood of 44 Tested Citizens of Vareš: Despite the Alarming Situation ZDK Authorities Are Not Commenting," N1, December 18, 2025, https://n1info.ba/vijesti/kod-44-testirana-gradjanina-varesa-pronadjeno-olovo-u-krvi-uprkos-alarmantnoj-situaciji-vlasti-zdk-se-ne-oglasavaju/.

152 ***In October 2022, Hajrija reported the mining venture:*** Council of Europe, "Possible Negative Impact of Mining Activities in Trstionica–Gornja Bukovica and Vareš," July 2022, https://www.coe.int/en/web/bern-convention/-/possible-negative-impact-of-mining-activities-in-trstionica-gornja-bukovica-and-vare%C5%A1.

152 Hajrija's complaint to the Standing Committee: Hajrija Čobo, "New Complaint: 2022/07. Possible Negative Impact of Mining Activities in Trstionica–Gornja Bukovica and Vareš (Bosnia and Herzegovina)," Council of Europe, Bern Convention, Convention on the Conservation of European Wildlife and Natural Habitats, November 21, 2022, https://rm.coe.int/files76-2022-mines-bosnia-herzegovina-complaint-form/1680ab9e31.

153 She went on to argue that the mining activities: Čobo, "New Complaint: 2022/07."

153 The Bern Convention committee met in September 2023: "Meeting of the Bureau: 12–13 September, 2023," Council of Europe, Bureau of the Standing Committee to the Bern Convention, Convention on the Conservation of European Wildlife and Natural Habitats, October 3, 2023, https://rm.coe.int/tpvs25-2023-report-2nd-bureau-meeting-12-13-sep-2023/1680accb13.

154 "The works are carried out on a hill with a water system": Ibro Čavčić, "The Zenica Government Treat for the World's Ore Traders," Center for Investigative Reporting (CIN), July 12, 2023, https://cin.ba/en/the-zenica-government-treat-for-the-worlds-ore-traders/.

155 In April 2024, the company abruptly withdrew the lawsuit: "Hajrija Čobo: Targeted for Speaking Out about the Impacts of Mining in Bosnia and Herzegovina," Stop the Persecution!, https://stop-persecution.org/hajrija-cobo-targeted-for-speaking-out-about-the-impacts-of-mining-in-bosnia-and-herzegovina.

156 The international NGO Front Line Defenders publicized her case: "Hajrija Čobo: HRD, Environmental Rights Defender," Front Line Defenders, https://www.frontlinedefenders.org/en/profile/hajrija-cobo.

156 Mary Lawlor visited Hajrija: Mary Lawlor (@MaryLawlorHRDs), UN Special Rapporteur for Human Rights Defenders, "Day 9 of My

Country Visit, I Travelled to Kakanj," Facebook, June 18, 2025, https://www.facebook.com/MaryLawlorHRDs/posts/1168093785335457.

156 An October 2023 complaint about Adriatic Metals: Sanja Mlađenović Stević, "In Bosnia, a Mine Is Devastating Forests and Dividing the Country," Voxeurop, July 22, 2025, https://voxeurop.eu/en/bosnia-mine-devastating-forests-dividing-country/.

156 However, the Constitutional Court ruling was never implemented: Marija Augustinovic and Milorad Milojevic, Radio Slobodna Evropa, "Constitutional Court Overturns Permission Granted to Adriatic Metals to Clear State-Owned Forests for Mining; Co. Allegedly Ignores Ruling," Business and Human Rights Centre, January 29, 2024, https://www.business-humanrights.org/en/latest-news/bosnia-and-herzegovina-constitutional-court-overturns-permission-granted-to-adriatic-metals-to-clear-state-owned-forests-for-mining-co-allegedly-ignores-ruling/.

156 In December 2024, a regional court annulled the permit: "Adriatic Metals Loses Mining License in Vareš," Center for Investigative Reporting (CIN), January 16, 2025, https://cin.ba/en/adriatic-metals-loses-mining-license-in-vares/.

157 the national government issued a brand new authorization: "Adriatic Metals Fast-Tracks New Mining Permit," Center for Investigative Reporting (CIN), February 11, 2025, https://cin.ba/en/adriatic-metals-fast-tracks-new-mining-permit/.

157 Rae promised that DPM would "optimize": "Dundee Precious Metals Completes Acquisition of Adriatic Metals and Confirms Name Change and ASX Listing," DPM Metals, September 3, 2025, https://dpmmetals.com/news-media/news-releases/dundee-precious-metals-completes-acquisition-of-ad-10963/

157 Bosnia and Herzegovina rated 109th out of 182: "Corruptions Perceptions Index, 2025," https://www.transparency.org/en/cpi/2025.

157–58 The municipality's population dropped: "Kakanj," City Population, August 20, 2023, https://www.citypopulation.de/en/bosnia/admin/federacija_bosna_i_herceg/10448__kakanj.

Chapter 11:

164 An infamous troll farm: "RBC Investigation: How the 'Troll Factory' Operated the US Elections," RBC, October 17, 2017, https://www.rbc.ru/magazine/2017/11/59e0c17d9a79470e05a9e6c1.

165 He was expected to produce 135 online commentaries: Sandra Ifraimova, "A Former Russian Troll Explains How to Spread Fake News," *Time,* February 21, 2018, updated December 12, 2023, https://time.com/5168202/russia-troll-internet-research-agency/.

165 According to a researcher on Russia: Dana Nickel, "Russia Is Quietly Churning Out Fake Content Posing as US News," *Politico,* August 17, 2025, https://www.politico.com/news/2025/08/17/russia-us-news-media-disinformation-campaign-00512173.

165 Incredibly, a March 2022 YouGov/*Economist *poll: "Which Groups of Americans Believe Conspiracy Theories about Ukraine and Russia?," YouGov, March 30, 2022, https://today.yougov.com/politics/articles/41874-which-groups-believe-conspiracies-ukraine-russia.

165 a false story believed to have come from pro-Kremlin trolls: Teri Schultz, "Lithuania Pushes Back on Fake News," Deutsche Welle, February 23, 2017, https://www.dw.com/en/why-the-fake-rape-story-against-german-nato-forces-fell-flat-in-lithuania/a-37694870.

165 a fake tweet from then-US Secretary of State Mike Pompeo: Madeline Roache, "Lithuania Fights Info War as It Marks Independence Anniversary," Al Jazeera, March 11, 2020, https://www.aljazeera.com/features/2020/3/11/lithuania-fights-info-war-as-it-marks-independence-anniversary.

165 In May 2025, rumors were spread across social media: "Lithuania Warns of Russian Fake News Over Locals 'Fleeing' Strategic Border Area," TVP World, May 29, 2025, https://tvpworld.com/86983503/lithuania-warns-of-russian-fake-news-over-locals-fleeing.

165 this shift "meant freedom": Andrei Kolesnikov, "Gorbachev's Revolution," Carnegie Russia Eurasia Center, *Carnegie Politika*, August 31, 2022, https://carnegieendowment.org/russia-eurasia/politika/2022/08/gorbachevs-revolution.

172 Over several years, I have extensively documented attacks on Kharkiv: Brian Dooley, "Bombed Out and Occupied: Russia's Invasion of Izyum," Human Rights First, June 28, 2023, https://humanrightsfirst.org/library/bombed-out-and-occupied-russias-invasion-of-izyum/.

173 The US-based think tank Atlantic Council: https://atlanticcouncil.org/wp-content/uploads/2023/06/scaling-trust-on-the-web_annex6.pdf

173 NewsGuard, an organization that: https://www.newsguardtech.com/insights/watch-out-ai-news-sites-are-on-the-rise/

174 the rise of technology would destroy more jobs: Katie Allen, "Technology Has Created More Jobs Than It Has Destroyed, Says 140 Years of Data," *Guardian*, August 18, 2015, https://www.theguardian.com/business/2015/aug/17/technology-created-more-jobs-than-destroyed-140-years-data-census.

174 texting would kill language: John McWhorter, "Is Texting Killing the English Language?," *Time*, April 25, 2013, https://ideas.time.com/2013/04/25/is-texting-killing-the-english-language/.

174 Finland consistently ranks first: Open Society Institute—Sofia, "'Bye, Bye, Birdie'": Meeting the Challenges of Disinformation," Media Literacy Index 2023, June 2023, https://osis.bg/wp-content/uploads/2023/06/MLI-report-in-English-22.06.pdf.